About the Author

Matt Wingett is a writer and public speaker with a love of literat.
former scriptwriter on ITV's police show *The Bill*, he has written short stories, articles for the national press and also works as an advertising copywriter.

Over the years, he has encountered Portsmouth in literature and art, and has been inspired to write about the city's rich literary heritage.

His interest in former Portsmouth citizen Sir Arthur Conan Doyle led him to write *Conan Doyle and the Mysterious World of Light, 1887-1920,* an acount of the famous author's faith in Spiritualism, which was shaped by his life in Southsea. His collaborations with other writers and artists have produced works such as *Day of the Dead, Portsmouth Fairy Tales for Grown-Ups, Dark City* and *Pompey Writes.*

His novel *The Snow Witch* is set in Portsmouth, which he considers the perfect setting for fiction. It seems that many much better-known writers in this book agree.

THE RAILWAY STATION.

HIGH-STREET, GOVERNMENT HOUSE.

Picture 1: Portsmouth, from the Illustrated London News,
April 8th, 1882

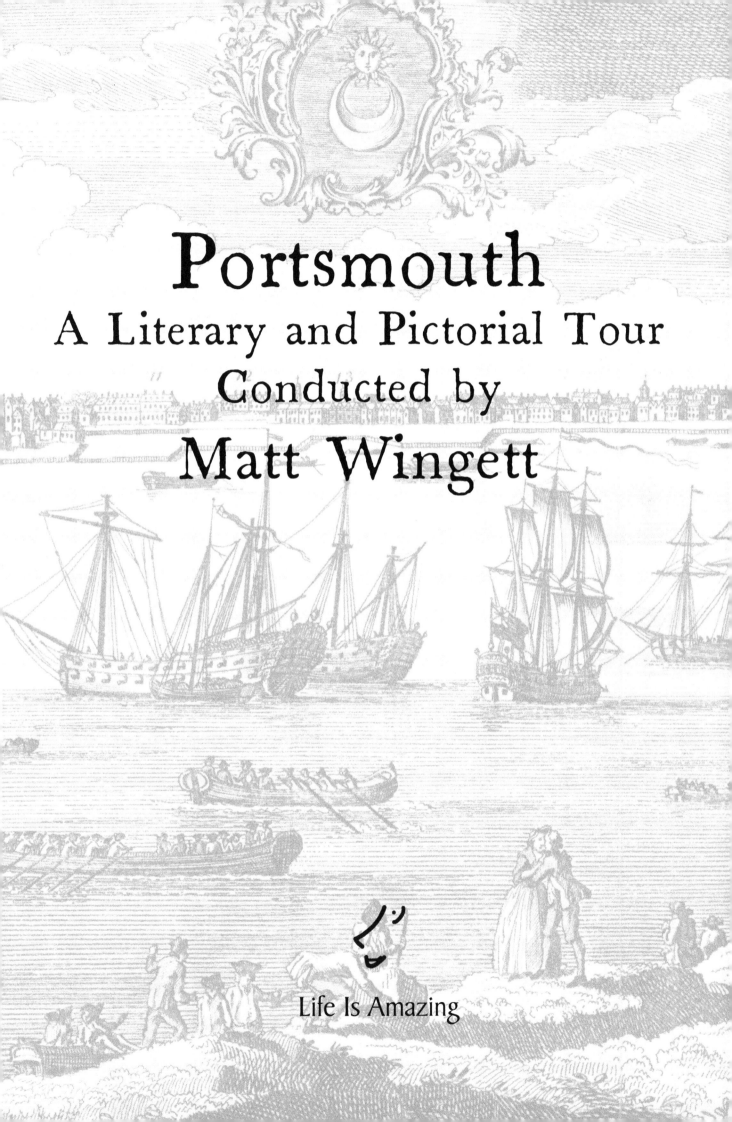

Portsmouth
A Literary and Pictorial Tour
Conducted by
Matt Wingett

Life Is Amazing

A Life Is Amazing Paperback

Portsmouth, a Literary and Pictorial Tour

First published 2018 by Life Is Amazing
ISBN: 978-0-9956394-8-5
First Edition

Introduction

There are numerous guidebooks to Portsmouth, and many more history books. They include excellent works on the city that will give you a whole bundle of great information on its environs and its past. This is not a history. Quite the opposite. It guides you through the things people have made up about the city.

It tells you how Portsmouth has appeared in the minds of people who've written about it and produced art about it, and in the stories people tell about it on the streets and in pubs. It's a personal tour, because it has got the things I like in it, some of the stories I've been told, some of the things I have found, or that I own, and some of my memories. So, let's say right now, it's not exhaustive and it's not authoritative. Some of it isn't even true. But anyway, I hope you like it.

Over the years, I've read some really fascinating accounts of Portsmouth and Portsmouth life - from W G Gates's *Illustrated History of Portsmouth*, through contemporary accounts of its citizens, such as *Recollections of John Pounds* and *Ten Years in a Portsmouth Slum*, to histories, such as Lake Allen's scholarly *History of Portsmouth*, old newspaper reports, the excellent *Portsmouth Papers* published by the City Council - and much more besides.

I've also encountered Portsmouth in stories, poems, novels and songs. Famous people have recorded their impressions of the town - among many others, Beatrix Potter, Charles Dickens and even Mahatma Gandhi had things to say about it. Writers have described it directly in novels. Jonathan Meades in his nightmarish tale of a dysfunctional family, *Pompey*, is one; from another era, Portsmouth-born Sir Walter Besant reveals himself as a fervent nostalgist for the Portsmouth of his 1840s childhood in his novel *By Celia's Arbour*; Captain Frederick Marryat makes the naval town come to life in his novel *Peter Simple* - while Rudyard Kipling hated it with a passion and describes the ill-treatment he suffered growing up in the town in his novel *The Light That Failed*, his short story *Baa Baa Black Sheep* and his autobiography *Something of Myself*.

Portsmouth has also appeared in disguise in many works. In George Meredith's novel *Evan Harrington* it is Lymport-On-The-Sea, or Port Burdock in H G Wells' *The History of Mr Polly*. Arthur Conan Doyle wrote about a doctor living in Birchespool in *The Stark Munro Letters,* drawing heavily on his real life as a GP in Southsea.

These are not the only writers to be inspired by the town. There is a whole crop of novelists and authors in the modern day who write about Portsmouth, or use it as a backdrop to their stories. More or lesser known writers such as Nevil Shute, Graham Hurley, Betty Burton, Lilian Harry, Diana Winsor, J. S. Law and John Sedden have all written novels that enjoyed mainstream publication. I have even helped bring some modern writers to the world, publishing books such as *Portsmouth Fairy Tales for Grown-Ups* and *Dark City* with their Portsmouth-rooted yarns, as well as the reportage of *Pompey Writes*. I've also published local authors from Portsmouth Writers' Hub who haven't necessarily written directly about Portsmouth, but are strongly connected to the town, in the collection of stories strange and macabre called *Day of the Dead*.

There is something special about Pompey. The fact is, people have things to say about it. Some see the beauty, some love the history, some hate the poverty, the dirt and the squalor of bygone ages. Some love and hate the same in the city today. There's no denying that Portsmouth was and is a lively place. In the past a massive military presence meant tens of thousands of young men sought pleasure and drink in its pubs and brothels. No surprise that fights, prostitution, drunkenness and debauchery were commonplace.

Perhaps this is why Jean Rhys, famous for the award-winning novel *The Wide Sargasso Sea*, sets the opening of her novel *Voyage In The Dark* in Southsea, where the story's central character first begins her slide into becoming a kept woman - and then towards prostitution. It's powerful stuff, and far cleverer than one 18th Century moralist who described the town's prostitutes as "Portsmouth Polls" with "Amazonian stature", "brawny arms", "warlike features" and such little sense of shame in broad daylight as to make "the great orb of noon to blush."

British hero General Wolfe concurred, commenting in 1758 on having to take up residence in Portsmouth while waiting to leave for Canada.

> "The necessity of living in the midst of the diabolical citizens of Portsmouth is a real and unavoidable calamity. It is a doubt to me if there is such another collection of demons upon the whole earth. Vice, however, wears so ugly a garb that it disgusts rather than tempts."

Writing as one of those citizens, I think Portsmouth gets a bad press!

Yet, others who came here have enjoyed the romance of the navy, the sea air and the bathing, and in later years, as Southsea boomed as a resort, millions of tourists came to holiday and enjoy the spectacles that occurred in the Solent. These included great naval reviews, military parades and other historical events - such as the Schneider Trophy, which many years ago a ninety-year-old neighbour of mine in Eastney told me she'd watched as a girl from the grassy banks of Lump's Fort on a glorious summer day in 1931. When she arrived home late, she told me with a smile, "I didn't half catch it from Dad. But it was worth it."

It isn't only writers, historic figures and the locals who have been inspired by Portsmouth. Artists, too, have answered the call. Engravers have pictured Portsdown Hill and Portchester Castle, painters have responded to the sea and Portsmouth scenes, and in a series of picture books I own, draughtsmen have captured the newer suburbs of Southsea just after they went up. Of course, there is another great art form from the late 19th Century onwards that found a perfect use in the seaside resort: photography. Photographs have adorned numerous postcards - showing not only the picturesque, but also the vibrant - such as thousands of dockers knocking off work and leaving through the Unicorn Gate. It was when I added to my collection of pictures the photographic postcards, the saucy seaside cartoons, and romantic holiday images I'd amassed, I realised I had a passable tour in the making.

This book then, takes you in a curve from the top of Portsdown Hill, via Portchester Castle, down the west side of the island where the oldest part of Portsmouth stands, turns east toward the newer suburbs of Southsea, doubles back, goes along the seafront, makes a mention of old Milton before taking you up the Eastern Road where you can have a beer by the sea, if you like.

If you do decide to do the tour, then you could take a car or bike from Portsdown Hill as far as the High Street Portsmouth. After that, you could do the rest on bike, or on foot, perhaps in parts. And to help you with that, there's a series of maps at the back so you can find your way. At the start of each section in the following pages are numbers corresponding to the numbers on the maps.

The book is filled with quotes from some of the many writers who've had something to say about Portsmouth, mainly in fiction, but some who've mentioned it in their personal journals and diaries - and to add a little extra colour, I also quote from travel guides gushing with praise for the town. I tell some of the local stories I've heard from Pompey people, some of my personal memories - oh, and I've even given some historical notes, for those people who expect a tour to do that sort of thing.

In between are the pictures, most of them my own personal items, some drawn from picture libraries. I've used them as points of focus for the quotes.

I hope this book entertains, informs and also gives you an insight into the town that you might not have had before.

I've included a bibliography at the end, in case you want to buy any of the books I've quoted from for yourself.

And since people have asked me where they can buy the images, the back also includes information about our catalogue. Each picture has a number, which is also its online catalogue number, so if you like a certain picture you can order it - many of them are available up to approximately A2 size!

I hope you like this book. I think it does Portsmouth (in all its occasionally rough, sometimes eccentric, often beautiful vibrancy) the justice it deserves.

Matt Wingett
Southsea,
Summer 2018.

Portsmouth
A Literary and Pictorial Tour

1 Portsdown Hill

Picture 2: "A view from the harbour and town of Portsmouth, with his Majesty's fleet under sail". A handcoloured engraving published by Laurie and Whittle of Fleet Street on 12th May, 1794.

Welcome! We begin our literary tour on Portsdown Hill: the great ridge of chalk downland that rises above the flat island of Portsea, with Portchester Castle at its feet.

Many authors and their characters have stood here, but let's jump back nearly 500 fictional years to the impressions left on a hunchback lawyer from Tudor times, C J Sansom's Matthew Shardlake:

We rode on in silence. The ground grew ever steeper as we approached the crest of the hill. We had almost reached it when we turned left. We rode along for a mile or so, through a little town, halting near a large windmill. We rode up to the crest of the hill and I drew in a long breath at the view.

Before us lay a complicated vista of sea and land. The hill descended steeply to an area of flat land cradling an enormous bay, the narrowest of mouths giving onto the Solent, the green and brown of the Isle of Wight beyond. The bay had a sheen like a silver mirror in the noonday heat. The tide was out, revealing large brown mudbanks. Directly below us, at the head of the bay, was a huge square enclosure of white stone that I realized must be Portchester Castle.

Heartstone, C J Sansom, 2010

In this part of *Heartstone*, Shardlake is about to make the descent into the town to uncover corruption at the highest levels of society, and to have a close brush with death on the Mary Rose, as tension mounts and intrigue winds around him.

It is a very different experience from that in the early chapters of Captain Marryat's novel, *Peter Simple*, whose excited young hero takes a trip to Portsdown Fair with his crew in a heavily overloaded dilly, or carriage...

At last, with plenty of whipping, and plenty of swearing, and a great deal of laughing, the old horse, whose back curved upwards like a bow, from the difficulty of dragging so many, arrived at the bottom of Portsdown Hill, where we got out, and walked up to the fair. There was Richardson, with a clown and harlequin, and such beautiful women, dressed in clothes all over gold spangles, dancing reels and waltzes, and looking so happy! There was Flint and Gyngell, with fellows tumbling over head and heels, playing such tricks; eating fire, and drawing yards of tape out of their mouths. Then there was the Royal Circus, all the horses standing in a line, with men and women standing on their backs, waving flags, while the trumpeters blew their trumpets. We walked about for an hour or two seeing the outside of everything: we determined to go and see the inside. First we went into Richardson's, where we saw a bloody tragedy, with a ghost and thunder, and afterwards a pantomime, full of tricks, and tumbling over one another. Then we saw one or two other things, I forget what, but this I know, that, generally speaking, the outside was better than the inside.

Peter Simple, Captain Frederick Marryat, 1834

Later, Peter hides from an escaped lion in its own cage - then rejoins his crew, who, realising they need to get back to the ship on time, set off a firework display early - with hilarious consequences.

Scenes of chaotic hillside revelry are also caught in Charles G Harper's popular history and travelogue, *The Portsmouth Road*:

When the ships came home (and ships were always coming home then), Portsmouth ran with liquor, riot, and revelry; and on fine summer days the grassy slopes of Portsdown Hill were all alive with the jolly Jacks engaged with great earnestness in the business of pleasure. Here, in the taverns that overlook from this breezy height the harbour, the town, and the distant mud-flats, generations of soldiers and sailors, fresh from battle and the salt sea, have caroused. Here, opposite the "George" and the Belle Vue Gardens, where "the military" and the servant-girls, the sailors and their lasses, still disport on high-days and holidays, with swings, Aunt Sallies, cocoa-nut shies, and, in short, all the fun of the fair, have the look-out men of a hundred years ago shivered in the wind while scanning the distant horizon for signs of Bonaparte and his flotilla, the inglorious Armada that never left port.

The Portsmouth Road And Its Tributaries,
Charles G Harper, 1895

For another denizen of Portsmouth, Portsdown provided a gentler form of entertainment. In the Reverend Henry

Hawkes' true account of the life of the Portsmouth educator, John Pounds, the children in his care accompany the philanthropic cobbler on long summer walks beyond the restrictive walls of the city, where they learn about nature, botany and geography. Come October, Pounds also walks to the hill alone, enjoying the view in a meditative state - including the one so often forgotten by writers.

> "October is a favourite month with Johnny. He likes to go over the Hill in October, to enjoy the rich autumnal tints in the trees. You may perhaps know, that from the top of the Hill, looking inland, there is a good deal of beautiful woodland scenery?"
>
> *Recollections of John Pounds, Henry Hawkes, 1884.*

When writers mention Portsmouth, the language is not usually so understated, as is the case with Jonathan Meades, in his shocking, dirty, joyous, Joycean novel *Pompey*, set in a bleak, bombed-out Portsmouth after the Second World War:

> That day Sonny drove slowly up to Portsdown, up and up, up trim roads of villas conjoined like Siamese twins, up roads that zigzag towards the sky, up gradients that grow so the engine wails with pain at the load and the slope, up to the chalk rampart and the serial fortresses on it, monuments to martial might and Palmerstonian paranoia and old salts' fear of Boney Frog. The world seen from Portsdown. Did you ever look down from Portsdown on a summer day when the rain was on its way? Ray Butt wasn't mad - stand where he sat, and look down: awe will strike, sooner or later. The coastal plain is a map of itself, full scale, *grandeur nature* and natural grandeur; The Solent, the three great (natural) harbours, the horizontal sea, the many greys of sea and land, the strata of refulgence, the solidity of haze, the density of water, the shimmer of the skyscrapers - all the buildings bend. And you are made to understand the necessity of water colour - the weather arrives in vast washes of every pastel Dulux would shudder at: pewters and gamboges, the colours of mould and charnel, of the seepage from dirty bandages. Now and again the sky is blue, or blueish, sky-blue even - but it's already reverting, showing off its protean spectrum of nameless shades, never-to-be-repeated hues (grasp it now, fix it retinally, it'll never come back so long as you live, this is your one chance ever).
>
> *Pompey, Jonathan Meades, 1993.*

My own remembrances are less grand than this magnificent writing from Meades. As a young boy, when I had my first view of the city from on high I couldn't process the idea of perspective. When my parents drove me over Portsdown Hill on the A3, I gazed at the tiny city below and wondered how so many people fitted into such tiny houses. From then on, and long after my brain adjusted to the idea that far away things look smaller, I referred to Portsmouth as *The Model Village*. Later, when I found out that it actually did have a model village, I recall having my mind slightly blown...

...A model village in The Model Village! Now that's just weird!

2 Portchester Castle

Picture 3: Engraving from "Portchester Castle, Its Origin, History and Antiquities", 1845

If we head from Portsdown Hill down Nelson Lane, we eventually cross the A27 on to Castle Street and come to Portchester Castle, the site of some of the earliest settlement in the area. What grand ambitions Portchester Castle had in its youthful days! Built by order of Roman general Carausius to repel Saxon raids, it was part of the Saxon Shore line of forts that protected the coast from Saxon marauders. When Carausius fell out of favour with Rome in 286 CE (it was rumoured by jealous rivals that Carausius's success in controlling Saxon pirates resulted from a secret deal), Caesar sentenced him to death and then recalled him to Rome. Weighing his options, Carausius decided to go it alone, and for a few brief years, a separate Roman Empire was centred on Portchester Castle, or *Portus Adurni* as it was called.

> He fortified all the harbours on this side of the channel; made Portchester his naval arsenal and chief dockyard, and sailing thence to the coasts of Spain and Italy, astonished the Romans with the first sight of the fleets of Britain. Meanwhile, he kept the coasts of Gaul so completely in fear of his naval power, that Maximian, the Lieutenant of Diocletian, who had thought to put him down with a strong hand, was fain to confirm the choice of the Britons, and to give his sanction to the supremacy of Carausius in Britain.
>
> *Portchester Castle, Its Origin,*
> *History and Antiquities, Anon, 1845*

Only when Carausius was betrayed by his treasurer, Allectus, in 293 CE did his reign come to an end. Allectus,

however, was a better treasurer than usurper, and in 296 CE was defeated by Rome, and Britain returned to the Empire.

I like this story of the earliest days of Portsmouth Harbour, when a brilliant leader stood up against an Empire, and for a few brief years, succeeded. It sets a defiant tone for this remarkable city.

That said, a more familiar remembrance comes from Portsmouth-born author Sir Walter Besant, who reminisced over childhood visits to the castle in the 1840s:

> Noone... can ever be tired of Portchester... On our annual visit we began by climbing to the roof of the keep and by walking round the walls and looking into the chambers; this done, we had tea in one of the houses outside the walls. There was no tea like the Portchester tea, no bread like that of this happy village; no butter, no cake, no shrimps comparable with theirs. After tea, we walked home - seven miles...
>
> *Autobiography, Sir Walter Besant, 1902*

Let's follow Sir Walter back, join the A27 and skirt the shoreline east, continuing on to Hilsea, where in previous centuries Portsbridge stood protected by the Hilsea Lines, which were the northern defences of the island. Much of them still stand today, with their moat and bastions now romantically overgrown in places, though their eastern end was demolished to make room for the now defunct airport.

If we cross over at Hilsea and follow the London Road, we eventually pass through the tight housing of Stamshaw - a greener version of which is briefly mentioned in a local poem from the early 19th Century:

> ...let us follow the sequester'd walk
> Through Stamshaw's verdant meadows...
>
> *A Metrical History of Portsmouth,*
> *Henry Slight, 1820.*

I like that line: "...Stamshaw's verdant meadows..."
Those were the days!

3 Commercial Road

Dickens used to live at the top end of Commercial Road, where his former home still stands. Many pictures of Dickens' house feature in postcards and books, so rather than repeat what so many have done before, I've included a picture of Commercial Road itself, from my postcard collection. Landport and Commercial Road are certainly areas Dickens visited in later life, even if he couldn't remember them from his earliest years, as this true account testifies.

> On the morning after our arrival we set out for a walk, and turning a corner of the street suddenly, found ourselves in Landport Terrace. The name of the street catching Mr. Dickens's eye, he suddenly exclaimed: 'By Jove! here is the place where I was born;' and, acting on his suggestion, we walked up and down the terrace for some time, speculating as to which of the houses had the right to call itself his cradle. Beyond a recollection that there was a small front garden to the house he had no idea of the place- for he was only two years old when his father was removed to London from Portsmouth. As the houses were nearly all alike, and each had a small front garden, we were not much helped in our quest by Mr. Dickens's recollections, and great was the laughter at his humorous conjectures. He must have lived in one house because 'it looked so much like his father;' another one must have been his home because it looked like the birthplace of a man who had deserted it; a third was very like the cradle of a puny, weak youngster such as he had been; and so on, through the row.
>
> *Charles Dickens as I Knew Him, George Dolby, 1885.*

In contrast to this gentle remembrance, a flavour of the ever-present underbelly of Portsmouth in the 1950s is caught in a remarkable novel from 1963, *The Red Sailor*, which starts with the anti-hero James Varne in a navy prison dreaming of freedom.

> Yes, sir. James Varne thought. The only place worth being on a night like this is in one those boozers down Southsea. Or in one those boozers on Commercial Road. Or . . . or any place really, so long as it's a boozer

you're stood in with one elbow on the counter and the other tipping bloody great wets down your neck. And Scotch Annie. Good old Annie. Big Lill too - the Bootnecks delight. Feet go where you like. I'm going home. And slapping those arses lined up along the counter. A grope at Lill too . . . no, you'd be hard put to grope that. And them looking at you that way when you came in - trying to guess how much you're worth because it is blank week and there's not a matelot alive got a bastard light. Give us a feel till Friday. Funny thing about arses. They don't look it but when you slap them it's like slapping a cardboard box. They're not all like that though. Just those wearing stays. It's the bones in them. You even see the bones poking out the way they stand sometimes. Same with roll-ons. Take them off and they got funny patterns imprinted all over them. Some those sadist fellows sit there all night with biros doing crosswords. Yes, sir. But you're not there tonight. No, sir. You forgotten what a wet tastes like. Even Big Lill. Though nobody should ever forget what she looks like. Thirty-nine more nights to go and all you can look forward to is sweating your bastard guts out thinking about boozers and wets and whores with cardboard arses. It's just your luck that the morning you get out this hole the Russians send along a little airplane to drop a bomb to blow the whores and boozers all to kingdom come before you even set foot on old Commercial Road. The only place left standing would be Aggie Weston's Rest Home and

her stood out front on the top step telling St. Peter how many Three Badge F.A.s signed the pledge the day before. Peace on earth and goodwill to all men. And the same to you with knobs on.

The Red Sailor, Patrick O'Hara, 1963.

Mention of Aggie Weston, or Dame Agnes Weston, reminds me of one of the many reasons given for how *Pompey* became Portsmouth's nickname. Dame Agnes, was the founder of the Royal Sailors Rest in Commercial Road (it later moved to Edinburgh Road), where she would sometimes give talks to sailors. At one, she described the murder of the Roman general Pompey, and a member of the audience exclaimed "Poor old Pompey!"

The story goes that this phrase somehow stuck to the city.

For me, it's not one of the more convincing reasons... but who knows?

General Pompey

4 The Tricorn Centre

Picture 5: The Cover of Architectural Design showing The Tricorn Centre, November 1966, (© Geoff Reeve, 1966)

From the roundabout at the top of Commercial Road, go right along the A3, keeping the Dockyard wall on your right. On your left is a large car park. This site formerly housed one of the most famous, notorious or infamous architectural icons in Europe (take your pick of the suitable adjective), The Tricorn Centre.

Opened in 1966, the Tricorn Centre was one of those buildings that people either loved or hated. When it was built, it was regarded as a shining example of brutalist architectural design. The idea was to incorporate all the needs of the community in a state-of-the-art building. There was space for a market, plenty of parking, shop units, a bar and even penthouse suites, looking out over Portsmouth. It was meant to be a bold statement about the future.

And it was, for a short while, until the design showed itself to be deeply problematic, and the materials used began to degrade. The concrete it was built from stained in the wet air, and large stalactites formed as the rain worked its way through the structure, leaching its strength from the inside.

Cars used to scrape down the ramps leaving gouges in the helical concrete ramps, and by the time I came to know it, there was a nightclub at the top called *Basins* where grimy rock bands came and played, isolated from everywhere else in the dark damp heights above the town.

Nevertheless, it had its deeply passionate admirers who were outraged when it was scheduled for demolition, which prompted this angry broadside from Jonathan Meades:

One can have nothing but contempt for the scum-of-the-earth councillors, blind planners and toady local journalists who conspired to effect the demolition of such masterpieces. One can only despair at the pusillanimous lack of support from wretched English Heritage.

The dependably crass Prince of Wales, the man who sullied Dorset with Poundbury, described the Tricorn as "a mildewed lump of elephant droppings", a simile as vulgar as it is visually inept. No doubt his heritage industry toadies removed their tongues in

order to chortle a moment's laughter. The critic Ian Nairn was on the money: "This great belly laugh of forms ... the only thing that has been squandered is imagination."

The incredible hulks: Jonathan Meades' A-Z of brutalism,
in The Guardian, 2014

DI Joe Faraday, the creation of crime novelist and long-time Portsmouth denizen Graham Hurley took the opposite view, however:

Pompey, he'd recently assured a visiting journalist from one of the broadsheet Sunday supplements, had at last shed its post-war reputation for poverty, planning mistakes and limitless aggression. This was no longer the city where a shopping centre - the Tricorn - was annually voted Europe's Ugliest Building. Neither were Friday nights infamous for sailor-bashing and huge helpings of recreational violence... Portsmouth, in short, was on the rise.

Cut to Black, Graham Hurley, 2004

I remember as a teenager coming out from the nightclub on to the car park in the wee hours to see a man lying on the grubby floor, paralysed by booze. He was the evening's designated driver and was slurring to his equally drunk friends "Just lift me up and get me behind the wheel, and I'll get us home." I hope they saw sense and called a taxi. I doubt he could have got them down the ramp in one piece.

Speaking of which, the Tricorn's unique design certainly had its uses. A friend told me how he used to go up it in the night with his 70-year-old granny, who had always wanted to skateboard. He would sit her on his board and push her down the car ramp to the sound of her excited whooping and laughter. It isn't quite the use architect Owen Luder had envisioned, I think, but I love it for its sheer Pompeyness.

Personally, I didn't hate the Tricorn for its looks, as many did. I reached a point after looking at it for a while where I began to see the intention in the design. It was just so alien from what many of us expected a building to look like that it took some adjusting to. But beyond that, its real problem was that it didn't work well as a building, with its damp and its dark and its barrenness.

And now it's gone - a more or less fond memory of concrete aspirations gone wrong.

architectural design

November 1966   Price 5s.

5 The Unicorn Gate

Picture 6: Postcard of dockers leaving the Unicorn Gate, c.1910

Carrying along the A3, we go from a former Tricorn to a Unicorn. The Unicorn Gate, is on your right hand side as you cross the junction with Unicorn Road. These days it is set behind the security checkpoint in the Royal Naval base, but you can glimpse it as you cross the light-controlled junction.

Here, we are close to the end of Charlotte Street, formerly called *Bloody Row* in the early 19th Century. Around it, numerous slaughterhouses and butchers sat cheek-by-jowl with residential houses, pubs and shops. Perhaps not surprisingly, Father Robert Dolling noted in his true account of his life in Portsmouth, *Ten Years In A Portsmouth Slum*, there was a continual incidence of typhoid fever here.

Dolling was sent to this part of Portsmouth between 1885 and 1895 to do missionary work. His first impressions of the town gave him a strong sense of its character:

My first Sunday afternoon, as I was walking in Chance Street, I saw, for the first time, a Landport dance. Two girls, their only clothing a pair of sailors' trousers each, and two sailor lads, their only clothing the girls' petticoats, were dancing a kind of breakdown up and down the street, all the neighbours looking on amused but unastonished, until one couple, the worse for drink, toppled over. I stepped forward to help them up, but my endeavour was evidently looked upon from a hostile point of view, for the parish voice was translated into a shower of stones, until the unfallen sailor cried out, "Don't touch the Holy Joe. He doesn't look such a bad sort." I could not stay to cement our friendship, for the bell was ringing for children's service, and, to my horror, I found that some of the children in going to church had witnessed the whole of this scene. They evidently looked upon it as quite a legitimate Sunday afternoon's entertainment. One little girl, of about eight, volunteered the name of the two dancing girls; she was a kind of little servant in the house, though she slept two or three doors off, and her only dread was that the return of a sailor, who had more rights in the house, might take place before the others had been got rid of.

Ten Years In A Portsmouth Slum,
Father Robert Dolling, 1895

Dolling worked tirelessly to close the brothels and build community spirit. He even raised the subscription for St Agatha's Church, the great redbrick basilica across from the Unicorn Gate, which rose above the squalid slums around it. The year it was built, he was discharged over disputes with his Bishop and was left with unpaid bills to the tune of £3,090 - the equivalent of nearly £400,000 at time of writing. Dolling cleared his debts by writing his book on life in Portsmouth, and going on a speaking tour in the United States.

St Agatha's aside, the rest of the area was devastated by a single explosion during World War 2, on the night of December 23rd, 1940. Known as the Conway Street Explosion, the blast was so destructive that rumours abounded the Germans had devised a new and devastating weapon. Though most agree it was an airmine, one older denizen of the town I met in the dockyard told me that when he was a boy he saw a German bomber pass over his house with its props stalled, and that it crashed with its payload still on board. He had been playing with Meccano, he said, and had gone outside to look at the raiders. His mother had gone to gather her kids into the cellar, but hadn't yet got them together. In the explosion, his brother was blown up the chimney by the blast, but saved by the frame of the chair he was sitting in, while the front door blew in and knocked his mother unconscious as she ran for the cellar.

Later, he said: "The windows in the house were all gone. But what I really noticed when I went into the living room, was that the lightbulb was still on, absolutely untouched, in the middle of all that destruction."

My own experiences are less dramatic. I can just remember Dad's car getting stuck at the Unicorn Gate as men poured through it on their bikes. We sat there for what seemed like forever, with Dad saying something along the lines of "It's just like China." It wasn't, of course, but at its height in World War 2, the dockyard employed around 45,000 workers. If you consider the amount of people then employed in supplying it with goods and services, the publicans who made their livings, and the prostitutes and brothels that did the same, then much of the island was dependent on the Navy.

Portsmouth writer Graham Hurley sums it up in one of his early novels, in which Portsmouth is sealed off by the government as the threat of impending World War 3 looms.

Once, the city had depended on the Dockyard, growing outwards, street by street, century by century, until tens of thousands of men regulated their lives by the wail of the Dockyard hooter. He'd seen the old sepia prints in the city archive, thin-faced men like his own father on ancient bicycles pouring out of the Dockyard gates: flat caps, roll-ups, and the gaunt certainties of life at the bottom of the pile. They'd watched an Empire come and go,

Men leaving Dockyard, Unicorn Gate., Portsmouth

these men, unquestioning, unacknowledged, badly paid, the perfect targets for disease, poverty, and - at the end of it all - the night bombing raids that had reduced so much of the city to rubble.

Graham Hurley, Rules of Engagement, 1990

The modernday dockyard has been a location for other novelists to exploit - from one-time Portsmouth resident Nevil Shute's early cloak-and-dagger yarn *So Disdained*, through Diana Winsor's spy thriller *Red On Wight* all the way to J S Law's gritty detective novels *The Dark Beneath* and *The Fear Within*.

J S Law makes an interesting point about the way Portsmouth wears its history so lightly, as he writes about Royal Naval Investigator Lieutenant Danielle Lewis returning there after an absence.

Portsmouth Dockyard... had grown and modernised. There were more cars and fewer people, but the layout was the same, and she relaxed again as they headed towards the cobbles of the Historic Dockyard, passing visitors and tourists on their way to the Mary Rose, or HMS Warrior; all hoping to see some history only a few hundred feet away from the modern warships that still had a hand in shaping it.

The Dark Beneath, J S Law, 2015

It is often forgotten that the dockyard also housed a prison that utilised what was essentially slave labour. One unusual but apparently true 19th Century account of dockyard life can be found in the anonymously written *From Prison Dock to Portsmouth Dockyard*. The confessional-style account of a man wrongly jailed for burglary describes the brutality of the regime, the crushingly undeviating pattern of life, the cramped cells, the hard labour - and the genuinely terrible food.

Six ounces of beef does not sound so bad, but a third of this is sinew and gristle, and those prisoners who have seen the meat carted into the prison yard resplendent in all the colours of the rainbow, with black and green in addition, may be apt to think that six ounces is as much as it would be safe for even a convict to eat.

From Prison Dock To Portsmouth Dockyard,
by An Ex-Convict, (c. 1890)

Prison is one of the many reasons given for Portsmouth's nickname. The French ship *La Pompée* was captured in 1793 and moored in Portsmouth as a prison ship. Interestingly, the Yorkshire term "Pompey" means *prison* or *house of correction*.

These days, the dockyard prisoners have long gone, and it has around 17,000 workers. The feast and famine of former times when Portsmouth was suddenly called on to provide ships and men to fight wars is now mostly famine. That's no bad thing, because that means peace. Yet even today, just under one tenth of the population of Portsmouth is employed in the dockyard.

6 Queen Street

Picture 7: postcard of Queen Street, circa 1900

Travelling past the Unicorn Gate and St Agatha's, we turn right into Portsea's main thoroughfare, Queen Street, which in former times was a notorious den of iniquity, just outside the Dockyard gates.

Quiet as it may seem in the daytime, there are few worse streets at night in the whole world than Queen Street, Portsea. I am sure there are no courts in the world worse than those which crowd around it. I am sure there are no characters worse than those which infest it.

Ten Years In A Portsmouth Slum, Robert Dolling, 1895

Personally, I don't think it's so bad, these days!

The town of Portsea first grew on what was formerly called West Dock Field, an open area deliberately kept clear of buildings by the army, whose job it was to protect the Dockyard from attack. When in the early 1700s, General Gibson, the Lieutenant-Governor of Portsmouth, threatened to turn his cannon on new buildings that could give the enemy cover, a deputation of shipwrights who wanted to live near their workplace petitioned Queen Anne, who was visiting at the time. Anne was persuaded by George, Prince of Denmark, to support their cause, and so Portsea began to grow. Queen Street is thus named in Queen Anne's honour.

Once a narrow street that lay within the massive fortifications that stretched in an arc from the sea towards Old Portsmouth, Queen Street was lined with pubs, brothels, naval outfitters and pawn shops. Little is left of the rumbustious street it once was, nor is there any of the tightly packed slum behind it that once housed prostitutes, dockyard workers, beerhouses and light industry.

The condition of Portsea in the early 20th Century scandalised polite society, specifically with the Blossom Alley murder, in which the hapless prostitute Mary Pelham met her grisly end in 1923, beaten to death by an unknown assailant.

Queen Street, Portsmouth

Her story appalled readers of the national dailies, as did reports of the awful living conditions in the mean, narrow, dank streets. In the years after the murder, many residents were rehoused, while the Luftwaffe helped with the slum clearance after that.

I have already mentioned the birth of Dickens at the north of Commercial Road, but Portsea's role in his entering the world is also well-recorded. It's oft-retold how in the early hours of 12th February 1812, Elizabeth Dickens went into labour while attending a ball at the Old Beneficial School, which is tucked away behind Queen Street on the corner of Kent Street and Curzon Howe Road.

The Old Beneficial School is now The Groundlings Theatre, and a few years ago I was given a tour of the building. It had been built to provide cheap education for children by the town's tradesmen in the 18th Century. Accounts of the severe disciplining of the children were thrown in for good measure, with tales of pupils bound and caned.

After this, our guide showed us upstairs to the former ballroom, now the theatre, and walked us to a fireplace, where he pointed to the floor.

"Here," he announced in a sombre tone, "is where Elizabeth Dickens' waters broke before she was rushed to Landport in a carriage, and gave birth to the greatest literary figure of the 19th Century."

We stood and looked at the floorboards reverently for a few seconds.

Then he added:

"We have mopped up."

Sailors Home, Queen Street, 1855

7 The Common Hard

Picture 8.: Postcard of The Hard, c. 1905

At the end of Queen Street, we come to the Common Hard, Portsea's waterfront, where Dickens' Nicholas Nickleby "stumbled upon two small rooms up three pair of stairs, or rather two pair and a ladder, at a tobacconist's shop, on the Common Hard: a dirty street leading down to the dockyard. These Nicholas engaged, only too happy to have escaped any request for payment of a week's rent beforehand."

The buildings in the picture opposite show nearly every one is a pub or inn, serving sailors and dockyard workers when they stepped through the gates. Charles Dickens' view of the area also shows an overwhelming naval influence.

Portsea is the most nautical part of Portsmouth. Here is the famous "Common Hard," where "liberty men" hasten to disport themselves; where few shops offer advances on prize-money and slave-captures; where the "Naval Rendezvous" invites men by bills to join H.M.S. Procrastination (wanting "a captain of the fore-top, a captain of the main-top, a good fiddler," and as many seamen as she can get), and where are several hostelries famous among naval men. Of these last is the "Benbow's Head," the favourite haunt of the junior and gayer part of the profession, while older and steadier gentlemen frequent the "Elephant and Castle." In the coffee-room of the former, a stranger will not improbably find a copy of the Admiralty's Gunnery Instructions, brought ashore by some youth who is "passing" in that science on board the "Excellent," and who combines with professional study a relish for pale ale. The youth is gone for a stroll, however, and the stranger may peruse at his leisure such examination questions as, "What is the first thing you do on getting into a rocket-boat?" (to which the reply in his case would seem to be, "Get out again!"); or, "Will grape penetrate the sides of a ship?" followed by the amplest information on the subject of red-hot shot. The talk at the B. H. is at once professional and playful, the well-known old mixture of smartness and shop. Charley Vivian was passing the college for navigation the other day, and when told that his latitude was only half the proper amount, gravely informed the authorities that he

THE COMMON HARD PORTSEA.

"forgot to multiply by two." Billy Sparkles has "missed stays." Tom Proby, by help of "a sweating fellow," has pulled through. It is much the same kind of talk one heard fifteen years ago; but the examinations are more numerous and more strict than in those days, a change which is making itself felt through the profession.

Portsmouth, Charles Dickens, 1859

At The Hard Interchange you might once have seen mudlarks going after coins thrown on the stinking mud flats by amused tourists.

As I sit here, waiting, I can smell the fresh black mud of Portsmouth Harbour. I can feel it round my knees, cold in summer, warm in winter. Clinging and pulling me down, as if it wanted me to be part of it. As if it wanted to absorb me.

I loved it.

Loved its feel as I waded through it. Slimy and gritty at the same time. Smooth and scratchy. It didn't want to let go of you when you came home. It stuck to you like a second layer of thick skin, and by the time you reached Jubilee Terrace it had dried into a big crust. As you walked home, you became aware of its weight. Gradually it crazed and broke round your knees and ankless and elbows and wrists

Mudlark, John Sedden, 2005

Countless true stories connect to The Hard, but one that sticks in my mind is that of the exotic crew member described in the memoirs of Captain Basil Hall, RN.

When Lord Melville, the First Lord of the Admiralty, to my great surprise and delight, put into my hands a commission for a ship going to the South American station, a quarter of the world I had long desired to visit, my first thought was, "Where now shall I manage to find a merry rascal of a monkey?"

Hall bought one in London, and brought it on board to keep up the men's morale while they were at sea. The exploits of "St Jago" or "Jacko" were soon well-known across Portsea, and his behaviour once the ship had sailed was both amusing and, Hall adds, "at times a real nuisance."

I need not dwell on the common-place tricks of a nautical monkey, as they must be well known to everyone; such as catching hold of the end of the sail-makers' ball of twine, and paying the whole overboard, hand over hand, from a secure station in the rigging; or his stealing the boatswains silver call, and letting it drop from the end of the cathead; or his getting into one of the cabin ports, and tearing up the captain's letters, a trick at which even the stately skipper is obliged to laugh.

Jacko was often used by the sailors to play pranks on the marines on board, but when he started biting the crew he

21

had his canine teeth nipped, something Hall obviously felt guilty about. After the ship was paid off, he entrusted Jacko to the keeping of the boatswain.

> This worthy personage used to place his pet in the bow of his little punt, as a boat-keeper, when he himself went on shore at Common Hard.
>
> *Fragments of Voyages and Travels, Second Series, Volume 2, Captain Basil Hall, 1832*

Of the lives of those many, many sailors over the centuries who came through the Victory Gate, drank, sang, loved, laughed, fought - then drank again, it's impossible to know much more than is written down in novels and true accounts of navy life. But a final image of The Hard as described by Walter Besant and James Rice gives a sense of the characters you might have seen there during his childhood in the 1840s:

> An open space gave access to what was called the "beach," being a narrow spit of land, along which were ranged on either side the wherries of the boatmen. A wooden bench was placed along the iron railing near the beach, on which sat every day, and all day long, old sailors, in a row. It was their club, their daily rendezvous, the place where they discussed old battles, smoked pipes, and lamented bygone days. They never seemed to walk about or to care much where they sat. They sat still, and sat steadily, in hot weather and in cold. The oddest thing about this line of veterans was that they all seemed to have wooden legs. There was, or there exists in my memory, which is the same thing, a row of wooden pegs which did duty for the lost legs, sticking out straight in front of the bench when they were on it. The effect of this was very remarkable. Some, of course, had lost other outlying bits of the human frame; a hand, the place supplied by a hook, like that of Cap'en Cuttle, whose acquaintance I formed later on; a whole arm, its absence marked by the empty sleeve sewn to the front of the jersey; and there were scars in plenty.
>
> *By Celia's Arbour, Walter Besant and James Rice, 1878*

8 Ye Spotted Dogge

Picture 9: The Death of Buckingham, Augustus Egg, 1855

Keeping the sea, the line of the railway arches and Gunwharf on our right, we come to St George's Road. Turn left, and you'll find the original Landport Gate that once let the traveller through walls with pointed bastions surrounded by moats with fortified islands called ravelins.

In Jane Austen's Mansfield Park, Fanny Price and her entourage approached the walled town at the Landport Gate, finding that they were:

> ...in the environs of Portsmouth while there was yet daylight for Fanny to look around her, and wonder at the new buildings. They passed the drawbridge, and entered the town; and the light was only beginning to fail as, guided by William's powerful voice, they were rattled into a narrow street, leading from the High Street, and drawn up before the door of a small house now inhabited by Mr. Price.
>
> *Mansfield Park, Jane Austen, 1814*

The experience would have been identical for Dickens' Nicholas Nickleby, 25 years later.

Once through the old Landport Gate, the traveller seeking the High Street turned left under the shadow of the walls and soon found himself at the top of a busy, crowded street. Here's C J Sansom's description of the 16th Century town:

> The street was unpaved, dusty from all the traffic, the air full of the heavy, cloying smell of brewing. We rode past tired-looking labourers, sunburnt sailors in woollen smocks with bare feet, soldiers in their round helmets who must have obtained passes into the town. A well-dressed merchant, a fine lace collar on his shirt, rode along with a pomander held to his nose, a clerk riding alongside calling out figures from a list. Like many others the merchant kept a hand on the purse at his belt.
>
> *Heartstone, C J Sansom, 2010*

If you are in a car and can find a parking space around here, this is a good time to get out and go on foot. There is a lot of walking ahead, and you may want to break this trip up into several sections. So, let's explore the High Street and Point on foot together.

Making our way down the High Street, just after the Grammar School on the left, we reach Buckingham House, formerly Ye Spotted Dogge, and prior to that Le Greyhound. The picture I have chosen is not one I own, but which caught my eye for its famous subject. Painted by Augustus Egg and exhibited in 1855, it shows the result of the grisly murder of the Duke of Buckingham by John Felton, which really happened just outside the inn on the 23rd August 1628, eighty-three years after Shardlake's fictitious 1545 visit to Portsmouth. Buckingham's death is told in fictional form in Alexandre Dumas's classic novel *The Three Musketeers*, but is more accurately described by a local historian with an eye for the dramatic.

The fleet being ready to sail, the Duke of Buckingham repaired to Portsmouth to take command. One Felton, a man of good family, but of a gloomy enthusiastic disposition, had served as a lieutenant under the duke in his Iate expedition to Rhe. His captain being killed in the retreat, Felton applied to Buckingham for the company; but being refused, he threw up his commission, and retired discontented from the army. The remonstrance of the Commons against Buckingham encouraged at once his resentment and enthusiastic fury; he was now convinced it would be a meritorious action in the sight of heaven to murder him, whom the Parliament had accused as the author of all the misfortunes of his country.

Filled with these ideas, he repaired to Portsmouth, fully determined to execute his murderous design.

Early in the morning of the 23d of August, Buckingham received intelligence that a small convoy of provisions had got safe into Rochelle; this news he communicated to the Duke of Saubise and the French gentlemen in his train, who insisted with great vehemence that the whole was false, and intended only to retard the sailing of the fleet. During these asseverations, the duke drew towards the door, and turning himself in the passage to speak to Sir Thomas Fryer, a Colonel in the army, he was stabbed by an unknown hand over Sir Thomas's shoulder. The knife with which the wound was inflicted reached his heart, and without

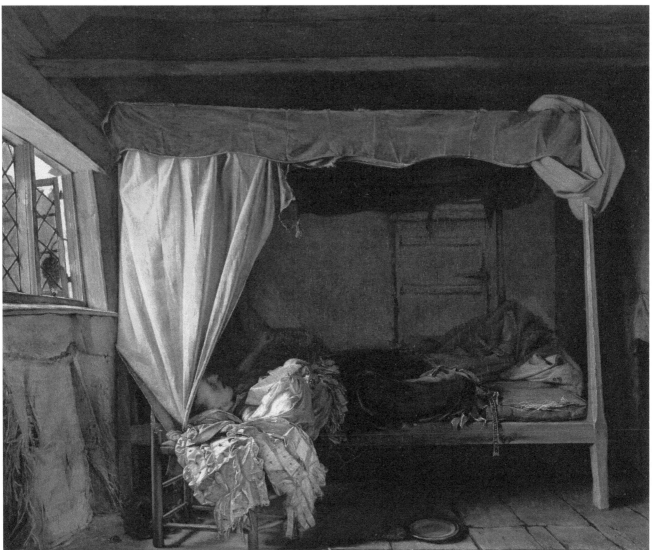

Image courtesy The Yale Center for British Art

uttering any other words than "the villain has killed me", he drew out the knife and immediately expired in a deluge of his own blood.

Lake Allen, The History of Portsmouth, 1817.

Recently, I had an extra piece of information given to me about that spot, when a man who grew up in Portsea told me of the *blood shadow*. "When I was a boy," he said, "a friend

used to point to the 'bloodstain' outside the house where Buckingham died – a dark shadow that would never wash away, forever reminding Portsmouth of that horrible act."

The Portmuthian told me they would gaze at it when it rained, and that it never faded away. I can imagine young schoolboys telling each other these tales with wide eyes and hushed tones, half scaring themselves to death as they looked down at a patch of motor oil on the pavement. I have to say, I've stood outside that house in rain and in shine, and have yet to see a dark stain that won't wash away. Bloody or not.

For many, a more indelible spot is the blue plaque next door, where PFC was formed in 1898, starting a cycle of agony and ecstasy that continues to this day as we follow the club's extraordinary journey.

I have to add, there is a myth that the great author Sir Arthur Conan Doyle was the first goalie for Portsmouth Football Club, and that he was present at its founding. Someone asked me about this recently, and (though it makes for a great story) sadly Conan Doyle had moved away long before PFC was founded. The team he played for was the amateur side, Portsmouth Association Football Club.

This answer gave my questioner some satisfaction.

"So, he definitely played for Portsmouth, then!" he pronounced with a smile.

And yes, you can certainly say that's true. Arthur Conan Doyle played for a team called Portsmouth, no word of a lie.

9 John Pounds Workshop

Picture 10: John Pounds Magic Lantern Slide, Anon, 1860s

A little way down High Street on the left is the John Pounds Church. Many Portsmouth people associate the name with the shipbreaking yard at Tipner, which belonged to another branch of the Pounds family. The original John Pounds was born in 1766 and worked as a cobbler in Old Portsmouth, or as it was then called, Portsmouth, since it still had something of a spring in its step. His story is fascinating.

John Pounds taught the poorest children for free to read and write during the early years of the 19th Century in his little cobbler's shop - a reconstruction of which can be seen at the back of the Unitarian Church just down the High Street on the other side from Ye Spotted Dogge.

Pounds went out in all weathers to find the waifs and strays, the orphans and the lowest of the low, many of whom were the by-products of the prostitution rife in the garrison town at the time. Those children, neglected and pushed out of their meagre homes while their mothers worked, would have ended their lives in crime, punishment, deportation or hanging had Pounds not given them the tools to take charge of their lives. He proudly boasted of his pupils that he "never had one hanged".

It is estimated that he taught around 500 children to read and write, 30 or 40 at a time crammed into his tiny shop off the High Street, down St Mary's Street, now Highbury Street. Were you to walk down there, in the early 1830s, you might well have encountered a scene like this:

On my way back to my lodgings in High Street, I had to pass the old cobbler's shop. As I drew near, I heard many children's voices, chattering and laughing all together. The upper half of the door was open, as usual; and his little tumbledown window was open too. Looking in:—there was the good old man in his glory!—in the midst of a host of little girls and boys, crowding about him, with merry laughing looks and voices! His birds seemed to enjoy the life and noise, and were singing loud. His cat was all alive, purring, and rubbing against the children. The old man, like a Father Bountiful among them, was sitting in his old arm-chair, with a large loaf grasped in one hand, cutting thick slices of bread, with quick alacrity, and spreading them plentifully over with butter; and then cutting them into halves, and giving the half-slices into the eager hands outstretched for them. He had no table; there was no room for a table. But on a shelf, close beside him, I saw a great tea-pot, and some mugs and cups, and a great sugar-basin heaped with sugar, and a great lump of butter beside it; and near them, there were two more large loaves in readiness, and another great lump of butter, and plenty more sugar.

"Has y' all got some bread-an-butter now?" "Yes, Mr. Pounds!" many voices at once. "No, Mr. Pounds, I'se not." "And I'se not, Mr. Pounds." "Two's not. I'se cut ye some, lads." And he cut another good thick slice, and buttered it plentifully, and cut it in halves, and gave it to them.

Recollections of John Pounds, Henry Hawkes, 1884

After his death in 1839, his example was taken up by reformists. The image I have included in this book is an idealised drawing taken from a magic lantern slide, used in the Victorian era to spread the word about his extraordinary work.

Pounds became the *poster boy* for the Ragged Schools Movement, and it was as a result of their work that England finally introduced Universal State Education. All of that begins here in a little cobbler's shop in Portsmouth.

A few years ago, I wandered into the Unitarian Church and was introduced to a lovely old lady, whe told me she was a direct descendant of Georgiana Richmond, one of the children mentioned in Henry Hawkes' biography of John Pounds.

Georgiana was best friends with another of Pounds' pupils, the wonderfully named Lizzie Lemmon, and together, they were were dubbed by John Pounds his "two queens". It was quite something to meet her great-great-great (I don't know how many greats) granddaughter, and to feel a living connection with the past.

As for the fate of the original shop, I once gave an old man I met at a bookfair in Oxford a lift to Portsmouth. A local historian, he told me how during the Blitz the shop was dismantled and put in the basement of the old museum on the High Street to keep it safe. Unfortunately, when the museum was hit, the firemen flooded the basement. After the war he asked to see the remains of shop. "All that was left was rotten wood floating in black water," he said.

Now he, too, is gone.

But I have his memory...

...and now, so do you.

The Landport Gate

10 Portsmouth High Street

Picture 1: *(frontispiece) Portsmouth High Street*
Picture 11: *Battery Row, hand-coloured engraving, c1860*

As we continue down the High Street, you can find an engraving of part of it in the bottom panel of the frontispiece, showing the Governor's House and the mad whirl before it, in 1882.

Portsmouth High Street was for most of its life a chaotic place. There are many accounts of it - and while I cannot include them all, a mention must go to Dickens' *Nicholas Nickleby,* who arrives at the Portsmouth Theatre that used to stand at the top of the High Street, and meets with local patrons as he accompanies Miss Snevellici as she gives *bespeaks,* or private performances in their homes.

For a flavour of the 18th Century High Street, here is an extract from Captain Marryat's *Peter Simple* to help us on our way. The spirit of the street, which was once a major shopping area stocking imports from all over the world, is captured in this extract beautifully. The story up to now, is that young Peter, a lad of tender years, has just arrived in Portsmouth. Wet behind the ears and with no understanding of what sort of a town Portsmouth is, he's soon accosted by a woman on the street, as follows:

I had arrived opposite a place called Sally Port, when a young lady very nicely dressed, looked at me very hard and said, "Well, Reefer, how are you off for soap?" I was astonished at the question, and more so at the interest which she seemed to take in my affairs. I answered, "Thank you, I am very well off; I have four cakes of Windsor, and two bars of yellow for washing." She laughed at my reply, and asked me whether I would walk home and take a bit of dinner with her. I was astonished at this polite offer, and I said that I should be most happy. I thought I might venture to offer my arm, which she accepted, and we proceeded up High Street on our way to her home.

Just as we passed the admiral's house, I perceived my captain walking with two of the admiral's daughters. I was not a little proud to let him see that I had female acquaintances as well as he had, and, as I passed him with the young lady under my protection, I took off my hat, and made him a low bow. To my surprise, not

only did he not return the salute, but he looked at me with a very stern countenance. I concluded that he was a very proud man, and did not wish the admiral's daughters to suppose that he knew midshipmen by sight; but I had not exactly made up my mind on the subject, when the captain, having seen the ladies into the admiral's house, sent one of the messengers after me to desire that I would immediately come to him at the George Inn, which was nearly opposite.

The Sally Port

I apologised to the young lady, and promised to return immediately if she would wait for me; but she replied, if that was my captain, it was her idea that I should have a confounded wigging and be sent on board.

Later after being admonished by the captain, he admits.

I cried very much, for I was shocked at the narrow escape..., and mortified at having fallen in his good opinion...

Peter Simple, Captain F Marryat, 1834

It was in the High Street, that the 17-year-old Beatrix Potter on a trip to Portsmouth in 1884 considered whether to buy dormice that were so large that she didn't believe they actually were dormice, agonising over whether she could transport them in a biscuit container. She was a little disappointed by the High Street, noting that one shop sold lovely old china that "suited my taste, but not my purse."

At 73 High Street, the novelist George Meredith was born in 1828. The son and grandson of tailors and naval outfitters, he was compared with Dickens in his day. Working as a publisher's reader, he was a mentor and friend to Thomas Hardy, advising him not to pursue his first (unpublished) novel because it would hurt his reputation. His instinct was right and he set Hardy on his path as a novelist.

Meredith was deeply admired by another literary resident of Portsea Island, Sir Arthur Conan Doyle. Meredith tended to focus on character rather than location, but in his semi-autobiographical novel *Evan Harrington,* his imaginary town of Lymport-on-the-Sea gives a flavour of Portsmouth people – the eponymous hero being the son of a tailor seeking to rise through society, much like Meredith.

The Town Hall of 1739.

Reticent about his connection to Portsmouth, the author later claimed to have come from "near Petersfield".

What, I wonder, did the town *do* to him?

Since we are discussing literary figures, another Portsmouth native, the 20th Century novelist Olivia Manning sometimes took tea at the George Inn, High Street, as a girl. With her father and brother, they would be shown the rooms where Nelson and Emma Hamilton slept the night before he left for Trafalgar. On such treat days, Manning would also be shown Dickens' house in Landport, where she would gaze admiringly at the gold lettering across the front door. The George Inn, like so much else, was destroyed in the war, and on its site now stands The George Court apartment block.

Like Meredith, Manning sought to escape Portsmouth. Her childhood in a town "on the outer rim of provincial ignorance" with a deeply critical mother who bickered with her unfaithful husband did not produce a congenial atmosphere for her creative soul. But before she left, she wrote three novels for *The Evening News* under the name of Jacob Morrow, which were published in installments, starting in October 1929.

Portsmouth very often took a drubbing from high-minded writers. The description of the town by Dr George Pinckard in 1806 is worth mentioning simply for his feelings of utter disgust at the place.

In some quarters Portsmouth is not only filthy, and crowded, but crowded with a class of low and abandoned beings, who seem to have declared open war against every habit of common decency.

His abhorrence of the town's denizens was levelled in part at the "Portsmouth Poll" prostitutes, with "red faces", "brawny arms", "two wounded cheeks", "a tumid nose", "scarred and battered brows", and "a pair of blackened eyes". But his disgust was also levelled at the tars whose business they sought.

Thus poor Jack, with pockets full of prize money, or rich with the wages of a long and dangerous cruise, is, instantly, dragged (though, it must be confessed, not always against his consent) to a bagnio, or some filthy pot-house, where he is kept drinking, smoking, singing, dancing, swearing and rioting, amidst one continual scene of debauchery, all day and all night, and all night and all day, until his every farthing is gone.

Notes on the West Indies, George Pinckard, 1806

Perhaps a little more on the positive side, the Georgian writer Charles Dibdin was complimentary about the good behaviour of prostitutes in the theatre on the High Street:

It is true prostitutes were seen there in plenty, there was a place set apart for them, where they were obliged to conform to rules and orders or be turned out. They did not dare to bar up the lobbies and insult modest women. Better discipline never was observed. They were permitted to be happy as long as their conduct was inoffensive, and so good an effect had this wholesome established regulation on their conduct, that, if I may judge by what I myself witnessed, there is more barefaced profligate indecency practised at Drury Lane or Covent Garden Theatres, than at Portsmouth Theatre in a season.

Observations On A Tour Through Almost The Whole Of England, And A Considerable Part Of Scotland, Charles Dibdin, 1801

It is to me a source of amusement that the scandalous town of Portsmouth has been transformed into respectable Old Portsmouth, now one of the more sought-after places, where daytrippers wander down to look at the art being created in the arches, and gaze out on the Spinnaker Tower.

Speaking of the Spinnaker Tower, in Alex Christofi's novel *Glass*, his central character, Günter Glass certainly sides with the locals as he cleans its windows:

I watched the people of Portsmouth go by. They were a good-looking bunch. I have often thought people are more attractive outside of one's home town – it's like you're on holiday, and you get that spontaneous, carefree sense that you might never meet again. Either that or I come from an ugly town.

Glass, Alex Christofi, 2015

With such reflections we arrive at Battery Row, overlooked by Charles I, who gifted the town with a lead bust of himself after he arrived here from an overseas journey on the 4th October 1623. The bust was situated in the side of the Square Tower (where a modern copy now sits) and residents of Portsmouth were expected to take off their hats to it as they passed – a habit they soon outgrew as the English Civil War (1642-1649) approached. There were attempts to revive this show of respect, with Viscount Wimbledon complaining bitterly in 1635 about the inn signs blocking the view of the monarch and the general disrespect of the crowds to the statue, but to no avail.

I like that detail.

A healthy disregard for authority despite being surrounded by symbols of it at every turn is something I think of as quintessentially Portsmouth.

11 The Saluting Battery

Picture 12: High Tide Below The Battery, by John Lynn, 1830s

A different type of salute gives the Saluting Battery its name. The battery fired cannon to salute important ships, and was also used to announce noon and sunset. It must have been a noisy place! We sometimes hear an echo of that sound as ceremonial guns crump across the city in the modern day.

You can see a lovely illustration of the seaward side of battery and The Square Tower with the now-demolished semaphore tower atop it in the picture, painted by John Lynn sometime around the 1830s.

The Square Tower was built in 1494, originally to house the town's governor, though later it was turned into a gunpowder magazine. I've already mentioned the English Civil War, and it was in the early stages of the conflict that the town governor, Colonel Goring, declared for King Charles I before he was fully ready to take control of the town. Thus, Portsmouth was soon besieged by Roundheads.

In response, Colonel Goring threatened to blow the Square Tower – and the entire town – to smithereens, unless he was granted safe passage. The Roundhead forces agreed, and Goring made his escape, throwing the key to the Square Tower into the sea as he did so. Locally-born children's author Percy F Westerman writes of Colonel Goring and his keys, thus:

> For answer Goring held up a large iron key which hung from his waist by a strong chain.
>
> "Dost see this?" he asked pompously. "I swear 'fore God that as long as I live the key, which is that of the Town Mount Gate, shall never fall into the hands of the King's enemies."
>
> "Amen," replied Firestone piously. "But how goes the garrison? Are the munitions and provisions like to last out?"
>
> "Powder and shot in plenty. Twelve hundred and fifty barrels of powder lie in the Square Tower, and two hundred in the vaults of the Town Mount..."
> *The Young Cavalier, Percy F Westerman, 1911*

For me, with its history of conflict, loyalty to the King and disrespect, the Square Tower is a reminder of the eternal battle between the haves and the have-nots - and also that history is an unstable affair made up of conflicting stories from which somehow a coherent narrative is formed.

As a lover of stories, I like it for that.

Keynote :

The key thrown away by Colonel Goring was eventually retrieved 208 years later during dredging in 1850.
But they had already fitted a new lock by then...

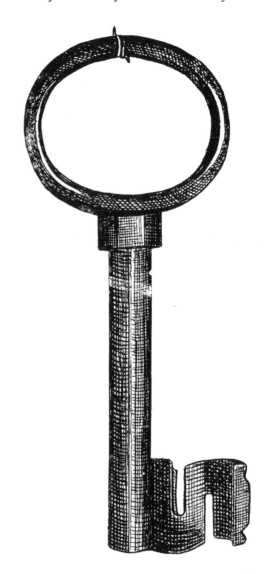

Extra Keynote :

The key was on display in the museum until it burned down in the Blitz. Who knows, maybe it'll turn up again in another 200 years?

High Tide Below the Battery by John Lynn, © Sotheby's 2010

12 The Hot Walls

Picture 13: The Queen's Yacht Leaving Portsmouth Harbour, The Illustrated London News, May 10, 1856

By the side of the Square Tower is a hole in the wall, the Sally Port where Peter Simple met his young lady. Stepping through it on to the beach we are suddenly near the scene of the picture opposite. The people of Portsmouth are crowded on the beach by the Hot Walls cheering the Royal Steamer *Fairy* as she leaves the harbour to inspect the fleet.

> It was a fresh and breezy day in March; the sun came out in occasional gleams, and shot long arrows of light athwart the clouds. The sea was dark with multitudes of boats, yachts, steamer, and craft of all kinds; the shore was black with the thousands who sat there watching for the signal to be given. And riding at anchor lay the ships on which the fortunes of England depended... Presently we saw the Queen's steamer the Fairy.... theading her graceful way swiftly in and out of the ships, while the Jack Tars manned the yardarms, and cheered till the shore took it up with echoes and the counter-cheering of the spectators... They sailed, the Queen leading the way. Out flew the white canvas, fluttering for a moment in the windy sunshine, and then, with set purpose... the Armada passed out of sight, and we all went home.
>
> *By Celia's Arbour, A tale of Portsmouth Town,*
> *Walter Besant and James Rice, 1878*

Charles Dickens was also present at a similar scene to the one Besant describes, during another royal visit to the harbour.

> While we are thus observing and moralising, there is a perpetual movement going on in the harbour, as constant as that of the tide. A lovely steam-yacht, neat and bright as a silver spoon, rushes in: it is one of the Queen's "tenders."
>
> *Portsmouth, Charles Dickens, 1859*

The contrast between the loyalists and those less in love with royalty is echoed in one of the rumours often told about Portsmouth - that Victoria disliked Portsmouth and its people. Diana Winsor's novel, *Red on Wight* states: "Queen Victoria didn't like the way they shouted at Albert and had a new railway line built to avoid it altogether."

True or not, Victoria certainly came to Portsmouth and people came out to cheer, as Dickens and Besant and this picture attest.

As for the name of the Hot Walls, this also comes from a time of broken loyalty. While it is true that on a summer's day the walls are a gloriously hot spot for anyone wanting to sunbathe, the name's origins go back to the Spithead Mutiny of 1797, when the fleet anchored in the Solent was seized by seamen sick of their mistreatment by the brutal Royal Naval regime. A number of mutineers were killed and their leaders (now in command of a fleet of fully armed warships) demanded the bodies be buried at Kingston Churchyard after passing in procession through the town of Portsmouth.

> The request was most positively refused by the Governor, and the town was put into position to repel any attack from the fleet, as the sailors were determined to carry out their plans. The batteries were manned and furnaces for heating red hot shot were got out and lighted along the wall near the Spur Redoubt (afterwards called the Hot Walls in consequence)...
>
> *Annals of Portsmouth, W H Saunders, 1880*

Thankfully, calmer heads prevailed and a compromise was reached, with the bodies landed at the Common Hard rather than in the town, with an immense crowd forming around the procession. The mutiny was defused only after the aged Admiral Lord 'Black Dick' Howe, who was trusted by the mutineers, was brought into the negotiations. When their demands for better treatment were finally met, there was much cheering and celebration in the streets.

Now, it's time for another one of those theories about how Pompey got its nickname. This one is all about the marching and ceremonies you would see in the town at the height of Empire. I can remember one old friend saying to me that when he was a young sailor, the people of Portsmouth would look for any excuse to wave a flag. One time, he said his commanding officer needed to get a group of men from Landport to the Hard, so he marched 200 sailors along Queen Street. By the time he'd got half way, people were lining the street, cheering - and, of course, waving flags. "We were only marching from one part of the town to another," he said. "But it didn't 'alf make you feel special."

This is why some people believe the name of Pompey comes from all its pomp and ceremony.

THE NAVAL REVIEW:—THE QUEEN'S YACHT LEAVING PORTSMOUTH HARBOUR.

13 The King James's Gate

∽

Picture 14: Liberty Men Returning – Engraving from the Illustrated London News, 1856

Back on Broad Street and along from the Square Tower, we come to the site of The King James's Gate, which marked the gap in the fortifications where the thoroughfare from Portsmouth let out on to Spice Island. The gate was built in 1687 as part of the walls that protected and constrained the town for centuries. The full defensive structure comprised a gate, a flooded ditch connected with the Camber Docks and a drawbridge. When you walk along Broad Street today, the bike racks under the cover of the Hot Walls mark the place where the moat lay, with the outcrop of stonework and solitary arch just before it all that's left of the gate's side wall.

Thus we head up to Portsmouth Point. Many people have theories as to why the area beyond the King James's Gate was called Spice Island. Some say it was due to the night soil carts that from time to time dug out the midden heaps and cess pits in the town. At night, they had nowhere to go, and so were parked up on Spice Island till morning – quite a *spicy* smell indeed! One eccentric local told me in all seriousness that the smell was due to eggs being thrown in the sea from a bakery, which I found interesting, but less convincing. Another told me that some of the ships coming in carried spices, and the seeds took root in the filth-splashed streets. Yet another told me that the ever-present prostitutes in this area made for a *spicy* night out.

What people always miss, though, is that with its moat across Broad Street, the area leading up to Portsmouth Point was indeed pretty much an island. When you crossed over water separating you from the rest of the town, you were in a wild, exotic, dangerous place cut off from the High Street.

That part of the name, at least, makes sense.

There is an engraving in the next section by Thomas Rowlandson which captures some of the roisterous nature of Portsmouth Point in the 18th Century. It shows people drinking themselves into a stupor, one gin-soaked woman collapsed on the floor while a man stands over her; a gentleman and prostitutes can be seen in the upper windows of the ale houses, while elsewhere two men carry a drunk woman off to who knows where. The whole is looked on by a fiddler with one leg, and it reminds me of a scene described by Walter Besant in his novel *By Celia's Arbour*, in which the young narrator witnesses the drunkenness for himself:

I was lost in the streets of the old seaport town... when I became aware of a procession. It was a long procession, consisting of sailors marching, every man with a lady on his arm, two and two, along the middle of the street, singing as they went. They wore long curls, these jolly tars, shining with grease, hanging down on either side below, or rather in front of their hats. Curls were the fashion in those days. There were about thirty men in this rollicking train. At their head, limping along very fast, marched my poor old friend Wassielewski, his grave face and melancholy eyes a contrast to the careless and jovial crew who followed him. He was fiddling as he went one of those lively tunes that sailors love, a tune which puts their legs a dancing and pours quicksilver into their feet. ...How was I to know that the Royal Frederick had been paid off that morning, and that a thousand Jack Tars were altogether chucking away the money in a few days which it had taken them three years to earn?

Laddy gets carried along by a sailor who takes pity on him:

...the man carried me tenderly, as sailors always do. We came to a public-house; that one with the picture outside it of the Chinese War. There was a long, low sort of hall within it, at the end of which Wassielewski took his place, and began to fiddle again. Dancing then set in, though it was still early in the morning, with great severity. With dancing, drink; with both, songs; with all three, Wassielewski's fiddle. I suppose it was the commencement of a drunken orgie, and the whole thing was disgraceful...

...Fortunately, at half-past twelve, the landlord piped all hands for dinner, and Wassielewski carried me away. He would return after dinner, to play on and on till night fell, and there was no one left to stand upon his legs.

By Celia's Arbour, A Tale of Portsmouth Town
Walter Besant and James Rice, 1878

All that drinking also supplies yet another reason for Portsmouth's nickname. "Pompey" some claim, is the slurred pronunciation drunkards manage when they try to say "Portsmouth Point!"

As a final thought, the King James's Gate still exists. Shorn of its curving decorative stone, the main body of the gate now stands just over half a mile away on Burnaby Road, by the United Services Recreation Ground – a gate that leads from nowhere to nowhere, through which countless boisterous souls with their untold stories, loves and lives once passed.

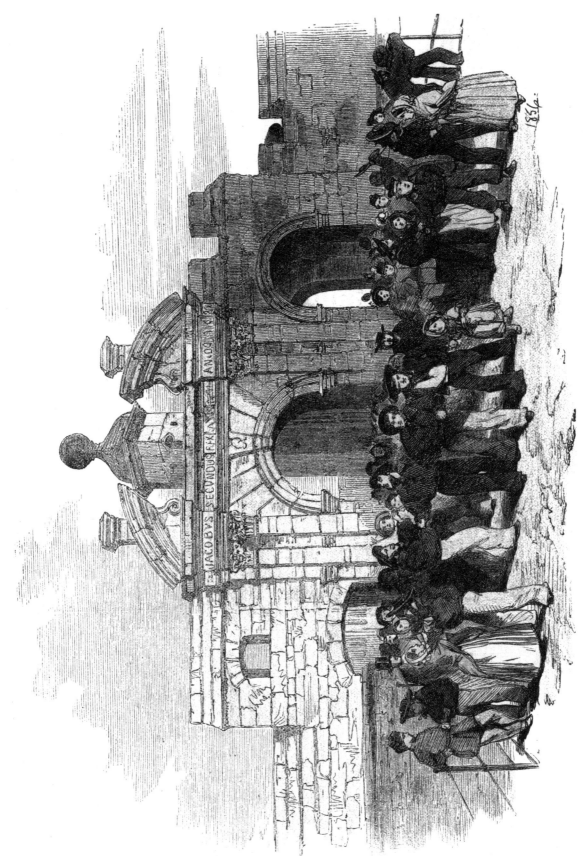

JAMES GATE, PORTSMOUTH.—LIBERTY-MEN RETURNING.

14 Portsmouth Point

❦

Picture 15: Portsmouth Point, Thomas Rowlandson, 1814
Picture 16: Entrance to Portsmouth Harbour, from a painting by E W Cooke, 1842

Having reached Point, we can either turn back, or imagine ourselves going out on the water in a wherry, as our predecessors in Portsmouth once did. It is likely that another literary daughter of Portsmouth got into a jolly boat, boarded a naval ship and set sail for America from here. Susanna Haswell Rowson was born in this part of Portsmouth in 1762. The daughter of a naval officer, her mother died two days after her birth and her father left for America a few months later to work as a customs collector. Susanna joined him and his new wife in 1766 in Massachusetts, where her lively mind took great pleasure in her father's library. Taken prisoner with her family during the American War of Independence, she returned to Britain in 1778 to become a governess. She wrote unsuccessful novels including the critically well-received though unprofitable *Charlotte, A Tale of Truth*. Joining

a band of travelling actors, she performed across England and then emigrated with them to Philadelphia. Here she republished her renamed novel, *Charlotte Temple*.

The story of a misused and naïve young girl seduced by a British army officer took on cult status in the new United States, partially because it showed how dastardly the British were. By the mid-19th Century it had gone through 200 editions. It was the first American bestseller, and is still taught in American schools today.

Of course, Susanna was probably quite happy to set sail when she was a girl, but her hapless heroine Charlotte is already in a state of confusion when she comes to Portsmouth, in a very different condition from that of her creator.

It was with the utmost difficulty that the united efforts of Mademoiselle and Montraville could support Charlotte's spirits during their short ride from Chichester to Portsmouth, where a boat waited to take them immediately on board the ship in which they were to embark for America.

Charlotte Temple, Susanna Haswell Rowson, 1791

Another author to depart Britain's shores from Point was a writing superstar of his day, the by-then aged Sir Walter Scott. In 1831, the aforementioned Captain Basil Hall was given the task of looking after him while he waited in

Image courtesy Wikimedia Commons

Portsmouth to leave for Italy's warmer climes to improve his health. Hall's account of how the First Lord of the Admiralty, having been told by him that Scott needed to go to Italy, immediately put a frigate at his disposal is testimony enough to the high esteem Scott enjoyed. His presence in Portsmouth made quite a stir:

Though Sir Walter walked but little, and with some difficulty, he appeared to have no objection to seeing company. The Fountain accordingly overflowed all day long. Every mortal that could by any means get an introduction, and some even without, paid their respects; and during the last three days, when his spirits revived, he had something to say to every visitor. He declined seeing no one, and never shewed any thing but the most cordial good-will, even to those who came professedly to see the show.

Fragments of Voyages and Travels, Third Series,
Volume 3, Captain Basil Hall, 1833

There were other reasons, too, that people took to the water from Point. In the early part of the 19th Century, when a ship arrived in harbour it was immediately surrounded by traders, seeking to sell goods on to it and do deals for exotic items brought home by sailors. Below is a wonderful portrait of a female character who could be found in Portsmouth, very much in charge of her destiny: *the bumboat woman.*

The ship was scarcely anchored at Spithead when she was surrounded by numerous wherries, filled with people who endeavoured to make their way on board. Jew jostled Christian, and Christian jostled Jew – all the good things the town of Portsmouth could supply changed places with pea-coffee, sea-pies, lobscouse, and salt-junk. The bumboat women, who were seated in the stern sheets of their well-appointed wherries, blocked up with legs of mutton, pounds of butter, quartern loaves, beef sausages, and casks of porter, anxiously endeavoured to obtain the preference. A bumboat woman is generally a character; and to be a genuine species of her tribe she should not weigh less than fourteen stone: the nearer she approaches to sixteen the greater her originality. She has been a fresh-coloured pretty girl, with good teeth, much chat, and more assurance, and has in her time captivated the hearts of more than one officer; this she knows well how to turn to her own advantage...

... To be mistress of her art, she ought to be as perfect as Cramer or Braham in the knowledge of flats and sharps, and have a capital ear for music in the sound of guineas; liberal when she is sure of being profitably

repaid, cold as charity when that desirable end is in any way doubtful. She should have a smile like a cherubim, and an eye like a hawk, to enable her to look into the heart of the party she is about to trust, yet be able to give tick with a good grace and affability of manner, so as to make believe all reasonable doubt of you is a stranger to her soul. All these qualities will not constitute perfection unless she be well skilled in the contraband trade, and can smuggle spirits on board for the sailors, and cigars and silks on shore for the officers.

The Saucy Jack. A Blue Jacket, 1840

Perhaps, while we're here at Point, now is the time to tell a curious tale told to me by a university lecturer concerning Quebec House, which is just beyond the Still and West pub along the shore at Bath Square. Formerly a bathing house with sea-fed tanks in the floor, it was named to commemorate the victory of the previously mentioned General Wolfe in Quebec.

The story my lecturer told me was that after his death in action at the Heights of Abraham, Wolfe's embalmed body was landed near this spot in 1759. Sculptor Joseph Wilton was sent to make a death mask of the hero – after all, his likeness would have propaganda value for the imperial project. When the coffin was opened, Wolfe's face was badly decomposed. The official story is that only a rough likeness could be made. My lecturer told me a different story. Looking around his men, an officer pointed to a rating and said: "He looks a bit like him." So, this unnamed sailor's life mask was taken and the portraits used in many celebratory images and sculptures of the great General Wolfe in fact show an unknown Jack Tar's face. True or not, I like this story very much. It is oddly democratic, and shows how easily facts are trumped by propaganda. A lesson for our time.

I nearly forgot to mention: Portsmouth Point is cited as another of the reasons for Portsmouth's nickname. The story goes that when ships passed Portsmouth Point, the entry in the ship's log was *Pom. P.* - hence: *Pompey.* Navigational charts also use this abbreviation.

15 Portsmouth Harbour

Picture 17: The Gallery of HMS Calcutta, Portsmouth Harbour, James Tissot, c. 1876. (© Tate, London 2018)

On our pictorial tour, let's imagine heading out on the water from Point to view the harbour, just as the subjects of our next picture have done. This beautiful painting (not in my personal collection, unfortunately!) shows two resplendent young women with a young officer, gazing out dreamily over Portsmouth Harbour in a private moment: a chaperone between two would-be lovers. The capturing of the fabrics, the postures and expressions is exquisite.

When I first saw it, I was struck by a coincidence. A famous writer we've already met was also on board the *Calcutta* in Portsmouth Harbour. In her 1884 journal, Beatrix Potter writes of taking a boat around the harbour, and then:

November 12th, 1884... We got up on board the *Excellent* which was beautifully clean as usual, and a striking contrast to the two other ships, being full of sailors.

What funny people they are, like children, tumbling over one another singing, and one playing gravely with the ship's cat. Fine handsome men, and very civil. There were just beginning ten minutes for lunch, and as we went up some steps we were nearly run over by some twenty or thirty tearing along. I would think sailors never have sorrows, I did not see a single grave one.

The first thing to look at was the big tub for grog, we also saw the cooking and mess-rooms and store-place, all of which seem very well regulated, also the ship's tailor with his sewing machine, and the ropes in the course of twisting by an ingenious machine.

We crossed by a gangway to the second ship, the *Calcutta*, which is included in the title *Excellent,* and considered as the same ship. We had a very civil and intelligent guide who explained everything, showed how the guns worked...

The sailors were being taught to work the big guns on two decks. On the upper the guns worked most ingeniously on runners, but the older ones had to be pulled round with ropes amid great confusion and tumbling. The teachers were very sharp, and kept the men always on the move.

One gunner made a mistake and was reproved at full length. The class became suddenly serious and the head delinquent looked as if he was going to cry. They fired some caps, which made quite sufficient noise to be agreeable...

Beatrix Potter's Journal, abridged by Glen Cavaliero, 1986

Remember, when sightseeing in Portsmouth, just how many sightseers famous and obscure have gone before you!

16 Portsmouth Harbour, Again

~

Picture 18: Portsmouth Dockyard, James Tissot, c. 1877 (© Tate, London 2018)

Another Tissot painting catches the joys of sightseeing, and the romance of it, too. Comprising a group of three in a small

him, or perhaps his sister feeling like a gooseberry, we can't know. The joy of this picture is in making the story up - and seeing that universal look of flirtation and awkwardness on the faces makes it such a pleasure!

The picture reminds me of an incident in Jane Austen's *Mansfield Park* in which another group of three explore and flirt in Portsmouth, in this case Henry Crawford desperate to be alone with Fanny Price, but with that blasted sister of hers nearby...

Once fairly in the dockyard, he began to reckon upon some happy intercourse with Fanny, as they were very soon joined by a brother lounger of Mr. Price's, who was come to take his daily survey of how things went on, and who must prove a far more worthy companion than himself; and after a time the two officers seemed very well satisfied going about together, and discussing matters of equal and never-failing interest, while the young people sat down upon some timbers in the yard, or found a seat on board a vessel in the stocks which they all went to look at. Fanny was most conveniently in want of rest. Crawford could not have wished her more fatigued or more ready to sit down; but he could have wished her

Point, from the harbour, 1899

rowing boat among the ships in the harbour, it is an absolute peach in observation. The young woman on the left is clearly taken with her Highland soldier. He looks at her with interest and and they share a knowing intimacy. On the soldier's right, another woman also wearing tartan looks ahead, trying to ignore what's going on. Either embarrassed or annoyed, she has that distant look of wishing she was not there. Whether she is his fiancée from the north, a chaperone, an admirer who wore tartan because she wanted to show him she liked

sister away. A quick-looking girl of Susan's age was the very worst third in the world: totally different from Lady Bertram, all eyes and ears; and there was no introducing the main point before her. He must content himself with being only generally agreeable, and letting Susan have her share of entertainment, with the indulgence, now and then, of a look or hint for the better-informed and conscious Fanny.

Mansfield Park, Jane Austen, 1814

17 The Victory

∽

Picture 19: Portsmouth Harbour - The Victory Saluting Her Majesty, 1851

We find more sightseers in a boat in the next picture. This large colour engraving of HMS Victory when she was anchored on the harbour beside a rigging hulk reveals the extremes people in uniform went to when there was a drop of blue blood in the vicinity. Sailors have climbed the masts and adorned the cross-spars of *HMS Victory*, perhaps to get a good luck at the Queen as she leaves the harbour, or alternatively, to let Her Majesty get a good look at them. The sightseers being rowed across the harbour are perhaps also hoping to catch a glimpse of the yacht as it leaves.

Climbing the rigging was an important rite of passage for the young sailor, and had its traditions attached, as Peter Simple discovered when he sought to assemble his uniform.

"Mr Purser's Steward," said I, "let me have a cocked-hat and a dirk immediately."

"Very good, sir," replied he, and he wrote an order upon a slip of paper, which he handed to me. "There is the order for it, sir; but the cocked-hats are kept in the chest up in the main-top, and as for the dirk, you must apply to the butcher, who has them under his charge..."

...I thought I might as well go for my cocked-hat, and get my dirk afterwards. I did not much like going up the rigging, because I was afraid of turning giddy, and if I fell overboard I could not swim; but one of the midshipmen offered to accompany me, stating that I need not be afraid, if I fell overboard, of sinking to the bottom, as, if I was giddy, my head at all events would swim; so I determined to venture. I climbed up very near to the main-top, but not without missing the little ropes very often, and grazing the skin of my shins. Then I came to large ropes stretched out from the mast so that you must climb them with your head backwards. The midshipman told me these were called the cat-harpings, because they were so difficult to climb, that a cat would expostulate if ordered to go out by them. I was afraid to venture, and then he proposed that I should go through lubber's hole,

which he said had been made for people like me. I agreed to attempt it, as it appeared more easy, and at last arrived, quite out of breath, and very happy to find myself in the main-top.

The captain of the main-top was there with two other sailors. The midshipman introduced me very politely:— "Mr Jenkins—Mr Simple, midshipman,— Mr Simple, Mr Jenkins, captain of the main-top. Mr Jenkins, Mr Simple has come up with an order for a cocked-hat." The captain of the top replied that he was very sorry that he had not one in store, but the last had been served out to the captain's monkey. This was very provoking...

Peter Simple, Captain F Marry 1834

This business of Jack Tars climbing gives us yet another of the explanations of the town's nickname. The story goes that in 1781 some sailors from Portsmouth were in Alexandria and climbed the ancient monument supposedly dated to the time of Gnaeus Pompeius Magnus, AKA the General *Pompey* whom we've met before. These sailors thus became known as the *Pompey Boys* – as did every other sailor from Portsmouth. Finally, the name attached itself to the town, and not just the sailors themselves.

Likely or unlikely? You decide.

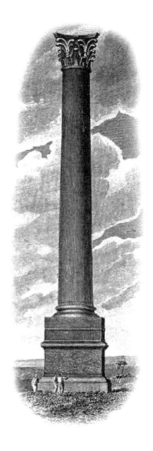

Pompey's Pillar, Alexandria

18 The Camber Docks

◦⤳

Picture 20: Portsmouth Industrial, Alick D Summers, c. 1935

Back on shore, a walk down Broad Street and a left turn brings us to the Camber Docks. A home for industry and commerce for centuries, one modern Portsmouth writer describes the sensory overload experienced there by his character Kitty Hawkins in 1832:

> She crossed the road over to the Camber Dock, stepping carefully over the sewage that flowed slowly down its middle. Soon the stench of excrement was overwhelmed by the stench of fish. The traders had been selling for hours, shouting lustily to anyone passing, "Fish! Fish! Luvverly fish!"
>
> *The Secret of the Scarlet Ribbon, Justin Strain, 2017*

For much of the 20th Century, the docks were dominated by the massive power station that stood near the present Isle of Wight ferry port. Fed with coal from the Camber Docks, smoke, diesel fumes and the sea were on the wind.

> A vaporous Solent gleamed beyond the lawns and trees of Southsea. The air tasted very slightly of oil from the Fawley refinery on Southampton Water, and perhaps a little of the smoke which was pluming gently away from the gigantic twin chimneys of Portsmouth power station round the corner.
>
> *Red on Wight, Diana Winsor, 1972*

The power station was decommissioned in 1977 and demolished in 1981. In recent years the area has been turned to residential use and increasingly gentrified.

It is easy to forget how industrialised Portsmouth was. The huge dockyard beyond Gunwharf was one of the world's most important sites of heavy industry for centuries, innovating in ship design, armament and weaponry. It even saw the creation of the factory assembly line, thanks to Marc Brunel.

I once told a Bristolian that Marc's son, Isambard Kingdom Brunel was born in Portsmouth. The information was received with stony silence. Then, he said through tight lips: "I think we can claim Brunel for Bristol." Perhaps, but IKB was *made* in Pompey, just like Dickens, who also witnessed dockyard industry firsthand, including Marc Brunel's blockmaking system:

The whir of machinery recalls the great factories of the north; and our senses are attacked at once by endless lines of brown yarn spinning itself thicker and thicker; men moving about with bundles which mysteriously begin to turn into yarn too; pools of bubbling pitch kept hot for the growing rope to pass through. Miles of rope of all sizes are made here on the different floors. Emerging, we see a batch of convicts harnessed together (a very dreary four-in-hand!), with such stuff as we have just seen making, and dragging along a huge piece of timber under the eye of a grim-looking task-master. "They sends the unruliest of them here," observes our policeman, "for they knows they're brought into order." Having looked at the Nelson - originally a hundred-gun ship, but never commissioned, and now being altered so as to be fit for a screw, which brief biography would do for more vessels than H.M.S. Nelson, apparently only built to rot - we enter a building where they are making blocks. This is a very pretty little operation, one of those neat affairs where machinery has its playful rather than its usual savage and triumphant air on. The pale, intelligent-looking mechanic takes up a bit of fragrant elm-wood; he makes the machinery whistle into it, and it is "bored;" again, and it is "morticed;" again (the circular saw hissing about it this time), and it is "commered;" a fourth time, and it is "shaped;" a last time, and it is "scored." A few minutes have passed, and the lump of wood is already a "block;" wanting little but the lignum vitæ wheel inside, on which the rope turns. The shavings accumulated by this process are capital as firewood, and used for that purpose (we were told) in the royal palaces as elsewhere.

Portsmouth, Charles Dickens, 1859

In the Camber area, excavations along Oyster Street show it was the original line of the waterfront. Docks existed from the earliest times, supporting small-scale trade and boatbuilding for centuries.

In more recent years, Clemens, Vospers and rival factions of the Feltham family built boats here. In the clapboard boathouse in one corner of the docks by Feltham Row small boats were built by George A Feltham, born in Broad Street in 1881 and still boatbuilding up to his death in 1975.

These days, boatbuilding of a different sort continues with BAR Landrover's massive shed that dominates the Camber Docks, where they produce cutting-edge yachts to race in the America's Cup.

So, the traditions go on.

19 A Right Royal Grand Parade

Picture 21: A Royal Interlude – Postcard of the Garrison Church with Parade, c.1910.

Now it's time to retrace our footsteps and head back along Broad Street. Passing The Square Tower on our right, we eventually come to Grand Parade, across which we can see the Garrison Church, the former site of the Domus Dei, where Charles II married Catherine of Braganza in 1662.

One of the many notables awaiting her arrival was the famous diarist Samuel Pepys, who split his time while here between administrating the Royal Navy, socialising, drinking and sightseeing.

(April 24th) No news of the Queene at all. So to dinner...

(April 25th) ...I was much troubled in the eyes, by reason of the healths I have this day been forced to drink...

(April 27th) ...back again by coach to Portsmouth, and there visited the Mayor, Mr Timbrell our Anchorsmith, who showed us the present they have for the Queene; which is a salt-cellar of silver, the walls of Christall, with four Eagles and four greyhounds standing up at top to bear up a dish - which endeed is one of the neatest pieces of plate that I ever saw - and the case is very pretty also.

Diary of Samuel Pepys, 1662

Portsmouth's Royal connections go back a long way. Portsmouth harbour provided an excellent haven for the fleet and Portchester Castle was a royal palace. Henry VI married Margaret of Anjou in 1445 over Portsdown Hill at Southwick. The Empress Matilda landed in Portsmouth in 1139 on her way to claim the throne of England. Unfortunately the usurper Stephen had the same idea, and the country was thrown into a 20 year period called *The Anarchy*. I never said grand ambitions always end well.

More positively, the first oranges to be recorded arriving in Britain were purchased in Portsmouth in 1289 for Queen Eleanor of Castile, Edward I's Spanish queen who missed the fruits of her native land. This story has been transformed by the power of myth-making into claiming Portsmouth as the first place oranges *ever* arrived in Britain. One assured expert told me this also accounted for why the British like marmalade, although the preserve is first recorded in Britain 400 years later. I love it when people make things up.

The most quintessentially English habit of all is a European import. Catherine of Braganza married King Charles II twice on the same day in Portsmouth, once privately according to the Catholic rites, and once at the Domus Dei according to the Protestant rites. She brought with her from Portugal several chests of dried leaves. Thus, the habit of tea-drinking became fashionable in England.

Queen Catherine leaves another legacy by providing one more dodgy reason for the town's nickname. Part of her dowry for Charles II was the Indian city of Bombay and some say that Portuguese seamen seeing a resemblance between the two ports called Portsmouth *Bom Bhia* – which to English ears sounded like Pompey. Personally, I think *Bom Bhia* sounds like *Bom Bhia* and *Pompey* sounds like *Pompey*. But hey, who am I to say?

As we keep the church to our right, and follow the railings up to Pembroke Road, I confess my own experiences of royalty in Portsmouth are limited. However, as we turn right into Pembroke Road, I do remember one misty night walking past this spot, and seeing a Range Rover pull up outside the Royal Naval Club, now on our left as we head east. Several tough-looking men got out and looked around, assessing me with a professional eye. I decided it best to cross the road, and, to my surprise, one of them thanked me. When Prince Edward got out of the car, the scene made sense.

So, that was for me the slightest of brushes with one of the Royals.

And I was only going to the pub.

(We are now leaving Old Portsmouth. We are about to start a longish walk. You may want to save the Southsea leg of the trip for another day - if not, let's go!)

Portsmouth

Garison Church Parade

2 0 The Pier Hotel

Picture 22: Pier Hotel, drawing, c.1890
Picture 23: "Spring Chicken" postcard, c.1920

When you get to the end of Pembroke Road, you are no longer in Portsmouth as it used to be delineated. Welcome instead to sunny Southsea!

The seaside town really started to come to life around 1810, when Joseph Croxton, a local entrepreneur, decided to build the beginnings of a resort, which he modestly called "Croxton". All that remains of that proto-Southsea is the name of Croxton Road, a short lane opposite the Holiday Inn. Nevertheless, the town of Southsea grew over the 19th Century, until by the end of it, one local writer eulogised:

> Many are the reasons which cause "all sorts and conditions of men," and women, too, for that matter, to visit Southsea. Some journey thither, wooed by the mildness of the climate. Others find unceasing pleasure in its social attractions, for nowhere is Society more brilliant. There are, in fact several Southseas included in our one Southsea. Naval Southsea is closely connected with the great dockyard and Portsea, and with the numerous "ships in harbour." Military Southsea is in intimate touch with the barracks, forts, and busy gunwharf. Artistic Southsea knows full well that there is no sea-scape that gives more variety of effect than the view of the Solent, with the Isle of Wight beyond. Commercial Southsea is keen and business-like, and nowhere are visitors better catered for. Historic Southsea finds ample material in the traditions and stories which hang around the comparatively modern borough, and ancient Portsmouth... Residential Southsea finds endless recreation during the summer, and a most genial climate in winter...
>
> *Mate's Illustrated Southsea, The Rev N Godwin, 1900*

The Reverend Godwin was laying it on thick for the tourists, but he had a point. Tourists came in their droves, entertainments were put on for them, and places were built for them to stay and enjoy the sea and the fresh air.

You'll see off to your left a building much like the drawing of the Pier Hotel opposite. Don't let the modern building fool you. It is a rebuild designed as student accommodation.

When I was a kid, I loved the old Victorian hotel in the picture, with its metalwork at the top of the steps, and an air of romantic age. It's funny how buildings become friends. Even as a teenager, I was saddened when I walked by that corner one morning to find the old place demolished.

Then, a few years later, I left town for a while and later came past to find it was back. I wondered if too many nights of beer and who knows what else were taking their toll. But no, I wasn't hallucinating. I thank the planners and architects for that building. It's a distinctive shape, and the rebuild was a sensitive decision. It slots right in at the end of the terraces beside it.

I've chosen the Pier Hotel to symbolise the numerous guesthouses, hotels and bed and breakfasts Portsmouth has seen over the years. Many, many people have stayed in the town at countless lodgings. For example, in 1890, a young and obscure Indian law student came to Portsmouth and lodged in a guesthouse somewhere in Southsea.

The student was Mahatma Gandhi, and he wrote about his life-changing stay later.

> It was in England that I first discovered the futility of mere religious knowledge. How I was saved on previous occasions is more than I can say, for I was very young then; but now I was twenty and had gained some experience as husband and father.
>
> During the last year, as far as I can remember, of my stay in England, that is in 1890, there was a Vegetarian Conference at Portsmouth to which an Indian friend and I were invited. Portsmouth is a sea-port with a large naval population. It has many houses with women of ill fame, women not actually prostitutes, but at the same time, not very scrupulous about their morals. We were put up in one of these houses. Needless to say, the Reception Committee did not know anything about it. It would have been difficult in a town like Portsmouth to find out which were good lodgings and which were bad for occasional travellers like us.
>
> We returned from the Conference in the evening. After dinner we sat down to play a rubber of bridge, in which our landlady joined, as is customary in England even in respectable households. Every player indulges in innocent jokes as a matter of course, but here my companion and our hostess began to make indecent ones as well. I did not know that my friend was an adept in the art. It captured me and I also joined in. Just when I was about to go beyond the limit, leaving the cards and the game to themselves.

God through the good companion uttered the blessed warning: 'Whence this devil in you, my boy? Be off, quick!'

I was ashamed. I took the warning and expressed within myself gratefulness to my friend. Remembering the vow I had taken before my mother, I fled from the scene. To my room I went quaking, trembling, and with beating heart, like a quarry escaped from its pursuer.

I recall this as the first occasion on which a woman, other than my wife, moved me to lust. I passed that night sleeplessly, all kinds of thoughts assailing me. Should I leave this house? Should I run away from the place? Where was I? What would happen to me if I had not my wits about me? I decided to act thenceforth with great caution; not to leave the house, but somehow leave Portsmouth. The Conference was not to go on for more than two days, and I remember I left Portsmouth the next evening, my companion staying there some time longer.

An Autobiography: Or The Story of My Experiments With Truth, M K Gandhi, 1928.

Today, we are not checking out in a fever of temptation. But we are tasked with a decision.
Down to the beach or into the 'burbs?

This place makes one feel like a Spring Chicken.

At SOUTHSEA.

21 Elm Grove

❧

Picture 24: Postcard of Elm Grove previous to 1897

Let's look for literary connections and mentions in the newer part of the city. Southsea's short history means it doesn't have the depth of associations that Old Portsmouth has. Even so, it has had – and has today – a host of extraordinary writers living here.

In *The History of Mr Polly* (1910), science fiction pioneer and superbly versatile author H G Wells based his fictitious Port Burdock on the Southsea where he once lived, borrowing the layout of "three townships that are grouped around the Port Burdock naval dockyards" as a model. Since we have already visited the other two townships, (Landport and Portsea), now its Southsea's (Port Burdock's) turn.

Let's continue up Southsea Terrace, with the Pier Hotel on our left, and turn left at the birthplace of the actor Peter Sellers on the corner of Castle Road, then stay on it to the junction with Elm Grove.

This road was originally named for the trees standing in its spacious villa gardens, before shop units stretched out to the pavements, and that leafy semi-rural feel of the road shown in the postcard opposite was lost.

Here we come to a hotspot for great writers. On your right is Bush House, the former site of Number 1 Bush Villas, where an impoverished Arthur Conan Doyle set up his practice in 1882, cooking bacon over the gas lamp in the back room and polishing his own brass plaque at night so no-one could see he had no servants. Conan Doyle's memories of Elm Grove are fond.

It was a busy thoroughfare, with a church on one side of my house and an hotel on the other. The days passed pleasantly enough, for it was a lovely warm autumn, and I sat in the window of my consulting-room screened by the rather dingy curtain which I had put up, and watched the passing crowd or read my book, for I had spent part of my scanty funds on making myself a member of a circulating library. In spite of my sparse food, or more probably on account of it, I was extraordinarily fit and well, so that at night when all hope of patients was gone for that day I would lock up my house and walk many miles to work off my energy. With its imperial associations it is a glorious place and even now if I had to live in a town outside London it is surely to Southsea, the

residential quarter of Portsmouth, that I would turn. The history of the past carries on into the history of to-day, the new torpedo-boat flies past the old Victory with the same white ensign flying from each, and the old Elizabethan culverins and sakers can still be seen in the same walk which brings you to the huge artillery of the forts. There is a great glamour there to any one with the historic sense—a sense which I drank in with my mother's milk.

Memories and Adventures, Sir Arthur Conan Doyle, 1924

While he was staying in Southsea, Conan Doyle wrote *A Study In Scarlet,* his first Sherlock Holmes novel, and was paid the not-so-princely sum of £25 for the world copyright. That was all the money Conan Doyle ever saw for it, but it brought him to the attention of a Mr Stoddart, an agent for the American *Lippincott's Magazine*, who invited Conan Doyle to join him for dinner in London, where he was entertaining an MP and a young Irish writer.

The other writer turned out to be a man who had already made something of a name for himself - none other than Oscar Wilde, who spoke praisingly of Conan Doyle's work. Over that dinner, Stoddart commissioned two historic books: from Conan Doyle *The Sign of Four,* and from Oscar Wilde, *The Picture of Dorian Gray.*

Now *that* is a literary dinner.

Meanwhile, Conan Doyle tended his Portsmouth patients as he wrote, including an elderly lady who would sit at a window and throw plates at passers-by in the street. How fascinating to glimpse the real lives behind the fame!

Not far along Elm Grove to the left lies King's Road, where the 14-year-old H G Wells arrived the year previous to Conan Doyle's arrival, to take up a position working in Hide's Drapery Emporium. It is intriguing to think that Conan Doyle and Wells may well have met in 1882, long before either were famous writers.

Wells, too, I have known long, and indeed I must have often entered the draper's shop in which he was employed at Southsea, for the proprietor was a patient of mine.

Memories and Adventures, Sir Arthur Conan Doyle, 1924

Wells' experience of Southsea was far less happy, partially because his mother persisted in placing him in completely unsuitable jobs, in this case, as a drapery assistant. He made light of his experiences in his fiction:

Mr. Polly was not naturally interested in hosiery and gentlemen's outfitting. At times, indeed, he urged himself to a spurious curiosity about that trade, but

Elm Grove, Southsea. Previous to 1897.

jws

Picture 25: Elm Grove Southsea

presently something more congenial came along and checked the effort. He was apprenticed in one of those large, rather low-class establishments which sell everything, from pianos and furniture to books and millinery, a department store in fact, The Port Burdock Drapery Bazaar at Port Burdock, one of the three townships that are grouped around the Port Burdock naval dockyards. There he remained six years. He spent most of the time inattentive to business, in a sort of uncomfortable happiness, increasing his indigestion.

The History of Mr Polly, H G Wells,1910

However, in his autobiography a more dispiriting and desperate life for the imaginative and browbeaten 14-year-old is revealed.

"Get on with it Wells." "Wells Forward." "Has anyone seen Wells?" "Sign!" "But you haven't shown the lady the gingham at six-three! The young man has made a mistake Moddum; we have exactly what you require." "A parcel like that will fall to pieces, man, before it gets home." And at the back of my mind, growing larger and more vivid, until it was like the word of the Lord coming to one of his prophets, was the injunction; "Get out of this trade before it is too late. At any cost get out of it."

Experiments in Autobiography, H G Wells, 1934

Wells realised later that his employers weren't bad people, but that they were driven to distraction trying to teach him a profession. He also wrote in his autobiography:

Although I tried hard and tried to school myself, the humiliating fact has to be faced by an honest autobiographer, I wasn't equal to the job.

Experiments in Autobiography, H G Wells, 1934

Wells hated his time working there. Due to a spelling error made either by Wells or one of his editors, the name of the shop is often reported as Hyde's, with a "Y" - a suitable revenge exacted by a writer for his unhappiness there.

I said that Elm Grove is a hotspot for great writers in Southsea. It is along this road, too, that a young Rudyard Kipling used to walk to school in the 1870s. If we turn right at the top of Castle Road and carry on east toward Albert Road, we are retracing his steps as he walked back through Southsea with heavy heart to Lorne Lodge, the house on Campbell Road where he stayed with his guardian, the cruel Mrs Holloway.

If George Meredith disliked Portsmouth, Olivia Manning hated its provincialism and Wells found the work tedious, Kipling takes the suffering of the budding writer in Portsmouth to new lows.

Kipling's parents were civil servants in India who wanted their son to have a British upbringing. At the age of 6, he was left in Mrs Holloway's care between 1871 and 1877, and the experience marked his life and his writing forever. In his autobiography, *Something of Myself,* Kipling refers to Mrs Holloway simply as *The Woman* and Lorne Lodge as *The House of Desolation*. He describes her unrelenting mistreatment of him in his short story *Baa Baa Black Sheep* (which is shocking, even today), in his autobiography *Something of Myself,* and in his novel, *The Light That Failed:*

Where he had looked for love, she gave him first aversion and then hate.

Where he growing older had sought a little sympathy, she gave him ridicule. The many hours that she could spare from the ordering of her small house she devoted to what she called the home-training of Dick Heldar. Her religion, manufactured in the main by her own intelligence and a keen study of the Scriptures, was an aid to her in this matter. At such times as she herself was not personally displeased with Dick, she left him to understand that he had a heavy account to settle with his Creator; wherefore Dick learned to loathe his God as intensely as he loathed Mrs. Jennett; and this is not a wholesome frame of mind for the young. Since she chose to regard him as a hopeless liar, when dread of pain drove him to his first untruth, he naturally developed into a liar, but an economical and self-contained one, never

throwing away the least unnecessary fib, and never hesitating at the blackest, were it only plausible, that might make his life a little easier.

The Light That Failed, Rudyard Kipling, 1895

Yet, in his autobiography, Kipling manages to draw something positive from the abuse he suffered in the house:

If you cross-examine a child of seven or eight on his day's doings (specially when he wants to go to sleep) he will contradict himself very satisfactorily. If each contradiction be set down as a lie and retailed at breakfast, life is not easy. I have known a certain amount of bullying, but this was calculated torture— religious as well as scientific. Yet it made me give attention to the lies I soon found it necessary to tell: and this, I presume, is the foundation of literary effort.

Something of Myself, Rudyard Kipling, 1937

It is along Elm Grove that Kipling, for another infraction of the rigid rules of the House of Desolation, was sent walking to school with a placard tied around his neck that read "LIAR". That many of his most famous later works such as *The Jungle Book, Kim* and *Captains Courageous* tell of an abandoned boy struggling in a harsh and alien world may indeed be down to his unhappy childhood in Southsea.

46   SOUTHSEA. — *Kings Road and Elm Grove.* — LL.

Picture 26: Southsea, King's Road and Elm Grove
Conan Doyle's House, No 1 Bush Villas, stood next to the Bush Hotel, right. The junction with the Kings Road has been straightened and the corner with Castle Road has thus moved.

22 Albert Road

Picture 27: Postcard of the King's Theatre, c. 1905

At the east end of Elm Grove, we turn right into Victoria Road South, then cross over and stay on the left so it forks into Albert Road. The view here is pretty much the same as when the photo was taken.

I've brought us here, not because Albert Road has a particularly literary past, but because it has a particularly literary present. As I write, modern Southsea and Portsmouth has a large crop of writers who perform in pubs on this road, write in coffee shops, meet and talk and share ideas... then scurry off home with their heads down and don't speak to a soul for days on end as their stories and poems unfold. We shall meet more of those living writers over the coming pages.

Of course, Albert Road also has its older literary connections. In an early novel by P G Wodehouse, it is to the King's Theatre that Lord Dawlish, AKA Bill, addresses a letter to his grasping fiancée, Claire, to tell her he's about to leave for America after coming into a million pound fortune. What he doesn't mention is that he is going there to try to give half of his fortune away.

He was guarded in his letter. He mentioned no definite figures. He wrote that Ira Nutcombe of whom they had spoken so often had most surprisingly left him in his will a large sum of money, and eased his conscience by telling himself that half of a million pounds undeniably was a large sum of money.

The addressing of the letter called for thought. She would have left Southampton with the rest of the company before it could arrive. Where was it that she said they were going next week? Portsmouth, that was it. He addressed the letter Care of The Girl and the Artist Company, to the King's Theatre, Portsmouth.

Uneasy Money, P G Wodehouse, 1916

It is the King's Theatre also, where Anna Morgan is working as a travelling chorus girl at the beginning of award-winning novelist Jean Rhys' *Voyage In The Dark*. An exile from the Caribbean, Morgan never feels either warm or financially secure in England, and the book is a brilliantly observed *fallen woman* tale with a very modern feel. Here she is, meeting her Southsea landlady:

Southsea, this place was.

We had good rooms. The landlady had said, 'No, I don't let to professionals.' But she didn't bang the door in our faces, and after Maudie had talked for a while, making her voice sound as ladylike as possible, she had said, 'Well, I might make an exception for this time.'

Then the second day we were there she made a row because we both got up late and Maudie came downstairs in her nightgown and a torn kimono.

'Showing yourself at my sitting-room-window 'alf naked like that,' the landlady said. 'And at three o'clock in the afternoon too. Getting my house a bad name.'

'It's all right, ma,' Maudie said. 'I'm going up to get dressed in a minute. I had a shocking headache this morning.'

Voyage In The Dark, Jean Rhys, 1934.

The King's Theatre was designed by Frank Matcham – one of the great theatre architects of the 19th and 20th Centuries. A cantilevered building designed to enable good views from most seats and with excellent acoustics, it started as a serious opera house, but it was soon realised that the way to make money in Portsmouth was to put on popular shows. The theatre was threatened some time ago with being turned into a pub, but the local community rallied round and saved it. Now it puts on first class shows.

A story I heard about its early days goes as follows: because the water table is very high here, and the theatre is built near the line of a submerged river, there were flooding problems below stage when it rained. Hence, a small boat was kept there, which duly ferried orchestra members to the pit in adverse conditions.

True, or urban myth? Does it matter? This book is dedicated to stories and storytellers...

There is a wonderful true account of what life was like at another theatre in Portsmouth – specifically the long-ago demolished Portsmouth Theatre that used to stand at the top of the High Street in Old Portsmouth, where Nicholas Nickleby performed with Ninetta Crummles, the infant phenomenon.

The quote below describes a scene witnessed by Georgian actor Edward Cape Everard, and sheds light on the aftermath of the sinking of the Royal George in 1782, one of the great maritime disasters that occurred at Spithead – of which I will tell more later.

Albert Road, Southsea. 42

When we re-opened, the boxes and pit presented to us a very sombre appearance; all as if it was a general mourning. On the second night, as though the gallery people were resolved to raise a laugh from the audience, which at that time, with all our efforts, we could scarcely extort ourself, they came pre-determined to have some fun; accordingly they did not want for ammunition; the came provided not with bags of black powder, but white flour; a certain number thus in the secret, they were to wait on the agreed signal from their captain, which I dare say they did very impatiently. As I've said, we played musical interludes and farces; our first piece was that night, "No Song, no Supper;" when *Lawyer Endless* was brought out of the sack, his black cloaths covered with flour, and the audience enjoying the scene, this captain, as they styled him, roared out, "My eyes but you shan't have all the fun to yourselves; hand some of it here." Upon which, he and his party, who were dispersed in the front seats of the gallery and side-slips, all at once emptied their flour bags over the ladies and gentlemen in the boxes, who instantly made as whimsical an appearance as *Endless* on the stage; this caused a confusion, and a roar of laughter from all but those who were annoyed; but they knew there was no redress, that the best way was to be quiet, so after looking at each other, they found themselves obliged to join in the laugh, and compose themselves as well as possible. From this circumstance, however, our boxes and pit wore their usually gay appearance, very few putting on black, fearing they should be saluted with a contrast colour.

Memoirs Of An Unfortunate Son Of Thespis,
Edward Cape Everard, 1818

Now, it is time for us to head back in the general direction of the sea, after stopping by at just a few more landmarks in Southsea.

23 St Jude's Church, Kent Rd

Picture 28: St Jude's Church, drawing, c. 1890

If we go back from the top of Albert Road and turn left down Victoria Road South, we pass the Portsmouth Temple of Spiritualism at number 73A. In the school building that used to stand here, Sir Arthur Conan Doyle was booked to give a talk on Spiritualism on September 6th 1919. However, finding an estimated 1600 people had come to hear him, he adjourned to the Portland Hall, which used to stand on Palmerston Road. On the following night he attended a séance, and believed he spoke with his dead son, Kingsley.

> Then came what to me was the supreme moment of my spiritual experience. It is almost too sacred for full description, and yet I feel that God sends such gifts that we may share them with others. There came a voice in the darkness, a whispered voice, saying. "Jean, it is I." My wife felt a hand upon her head, and cried, "It is Kingsley." I heard the word "Father." I said, "Dear boy, is that you?" I had the sense of a face very near my own, and of breathing...
>
> *A Wonderful Seance, Sir Arthur Conan Doyle*
> *Light Magazine, 1919*

Conan Doyle also returned to Southsea in 1926 to speak at a smaller gathering at the temple.

On our right, we come to Marmion Road, at the far end of which we reach St Jude's Church, pictured opposite. The Portland Hall where Conan Doyle addressed such a large crowd used to stand on the other side of the road, next to the Portland Hotel, at the top of Palmerston Road.

St Jude's Church was designed by local architect and mayor of the town, Thomas Ellis Owen, one of many architectural projects in Southsea, which included the building of the grand villas along Kent Road, and the streets behind it, renowned for their space and tree-filled gardens.

This is part of young Arthur Conan Doyle's stomping ground as he found his feet in Southsea in the early 1880s. An argument with the Reverend Charles Russell Tompkins from this church features in his autobiographical novel *The Stark Munro Letters,* in which he was already showing his unorthodox questioning of faith:

"You may label me as you like," I answered (and by this time I fear that I had got my preaching stop fairly out); "I don't pretend to know what truth is, for it is infinite, and I finite; but I know particularly well what it is NOT. It is not true that religion reached its acme nineteen hundred years ago, and that we are for ever to refer back to what was written and said in those days. No, sir; religion is a vital living thing, still growing and working, capable of endless extension and development, like all other fields of thought. There were many eternal truths spoken of old and handed down to us in a book, some parts of which may indeed be called holy. But there are others yet to be revealed; and if we are to reject them because they are not in those pages, we should act as wisely as the scientist who would take no notice of Kirschoff's spectral analysis because there is no mention of it in Albertus Magnus. A modern prophet may wear a broadcloth coat and write to the magazines; but none the less he may be the little pipe which conveys a tiny squirt from the reservoirs of truth. Look at this!" I cried, rising and reading my Carlyle text. "That comes from no Hebrew prophet, but from a ratepayer in Chelsea. He and Emerson are also among the prophets. The Almighty has not said His last say to the human race, and He can speak through a Scotchman or a New Englander as easily as through

a Jew. The Bible, sir, is a book which comes out in instalments, and 'To be continued,' not 'Finis,' is written at the end of it."

The Stark Munro Letters, Arthur Conan Doyle, 1895.

Now, let's move on from turbulent priests. Or in this case, turbulent doctors.

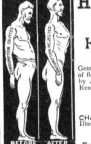

24 Palmerston Road

Picture 29: Palmerston Road, drawing, 1890s

Cross over from St Jude's and walk down Palmerston Road to find a transformed place. Once a classic British High Street, Palmerston Road was rebuilt after World War 2. Its wrecked state is captured by local author Lilian Harry:

> The shopping centre at Southsea had been virtually reduced to rubble, with the big shops Handley's and Knight and Lee's taking the brunt of the Blitz, yet, as Thursday said, there were still plenty of shops which had managed to stay open. Mostly, women were looking for household utensils which were beginning to appear again – pot scourers, wooden spoons, mops and china. It was all utility, of course – not bone china, Thursday thought a little critically, remembering the porcelain her father had made in Worcester – but it was selling in huge quantities. People had been making do with old china for years now, having to salvage whatever they could from their bombed houses, and it wasn't at all uncommon to be offered tea in a cup with no handle.
>
> *A Promise to Keep, Lilian Harry, 2003*

I bought some crudely-made balsa wood models of tanks from an antiques shop on Albert Road some years ago. They were made during wartime austerity, and I was told they had been salvaged from the wreckage of Handley's department store, at the bottom of Palmerston Road. I still have them, as a reminder of those dark days.

Lord Palmerston, after whom the road is named, was responsible for a series of defensive structures: the Portsdown Hill forts, and the massive Solent sea-forts toward which Palmerston Road points. Southsea-based writer William Sutton describes these latter structures (we will see them later) in the process of being built:

> The sun blazed on the bulwarks of the first fort, Spitbank.
>
> What an outlandish venture. Men, small as ants, busied themselves on the scaffolding that rose, glinting, out of the sparkling waves: like a house in a dream. Daring sailboats flitted around it, white canvas swelling in the wind. Beyond, the low inclines of the island were indistinguishable amid rafts of mist and cloud.
>
> Our destination, No Man's Land Fort, remained a ghostly outline.
>
> *Lawless and the House of Electricity,*
> *William Sutton, 2017*

I remember, when I first saw the forts in the Solent and my Dad explained what they were, I had no idea what he meant. Spitbank Fort, though, had a protrusion from one side and I became convinced it was the head of a gigantic Dalek buried in the sea.

Since Daleks are armoured killers, I had the right idea!

Spithead Fort, 1899

25 The Queen's Hotel

Let's turn right at the next junction of Palmerston Road, and head down Osborne Road. Just as Palmerston Road points to Palmerston's forts, so Osborne Road points toward Osborne House, the massive rural retreat on the Isle of Wight built for Queen Victoria. At its far end we come to the aptly named Queen's Hotel.

Picture 30: Queen's Hotel, postcard, circa 1905

The magnificent stone edifice dating from 1903, is where author and comic-book writer Neil Gaiman's child narrator meets with Al Capone's osteopath at a birthday party:

It was one of those plush seafront hotels... all red carpets, and marble pillars all veined and shiny. Beside each place was a cracker... We pulled them, carefully, because we were frightened of the bang, then we bickered over the ownership of the useless plastic whistles that fell out and put on the crown-like hats we found wrapped around incomprehensible mottoes. After the initial attack on the food, after the lights were lowered and the birthday cake successfully blown out, we were seated in front of the stage to watch the bald man come out with his thin balloons and pull billiard balls out of his mouth. I stood up and, unnoticed by any of the parents, I made my way behind one of the heavy red curtains at the side of the hall...

Violent Cases, Neil Gaiman, 1987

Here, too, Beatrix Potter stayed, in the older Queen's Hotel before it was remodelled into the one we know now:

November 10th, 1884... After wanderings in a Fly we finally settled the Queens Hotel which seems comfortable, a queer old house with mountainous floors. An ironclad is anchored opposite, and this evening the electric light has been dodging off it round the coast, the sea, and the sky, in a most erratic manner... A buoy opposite marks the sinking of the Royal George, at which one of the few survivors was a little child who clung to the wool of a sheep which swam ashore.

Beatrix Potter's Journal, abridged by Glen Cavaliero, 1986

The true story of the Royal George, at the time the Royal Navy's oldest and largest ship, is told by the poet Cowper:

Toll for the brave—
The brave! that are no more:
All sunk beneath the wave,
Fast by their native shore.
Eight hundred of the brave,
Whose courage well was tried,
Had made the vessel heel
And laid her on her side;
A land-breeze shook the shrouds,
And she was overset;
Down went the Royal George,
With all her crew complete.

On the Loss of the Royal George, William Cowper, 1782

This opening stanza captures the facts succinctly, but there was more to it than a nautical tragedy. It was also a tale of incompetence, arrogance and whitewash.

On the morning of 29th August 1782 while anchored at Spithead taking on rum provisions, HMS Royal George was heeled over to repair a minor leak. This was done by drawing in the guns from one side and securing them amidships, then running out those on the other side. With the ship tipped in the water, the carpenter was able to work.

A survivor of the disaster, Mr Ingram, takes up the story:

...by about 9 o'clock the additional quantity of rum on board the ship, and also the quantity of sea-water which had dashed in through the port-holes, brought the larboard port-holes of the lower gun-deck nearly level with the sea.

As soon as that was the case, the carpenter went on the quarter-deck to the lieutenant of the watch, to ask him to give orders to right ship, as the ship could not bear it. However, the lieutenant made him a very short answer, and the carpenter then went below... The lieutenant was, if I remember right, the third lieutenant; he had not joined us long; his name I do not recollect; he was a good sized man, between thirty and forty years of age. The men called him 'Jib-and-Foresail-Jack,' for if he had the watch in the night, he would be always bothering the men to alter the sails, and it was 'up jib' and 'down jib,' and 'up foresail,' and 'down foresail,' every minute. However the men considered him more of a troublesome officer than a good one; and from a habit he had of moving his fingers about when walking the quarter deck, the men said he was an organ-player from London; but I have no reason to know that this was the case...

As I have already stated, the carpenter left the quarter-deck and went below. In a very short time he came up again, and asked the lieutenant of the watch to right the ship, and said again that the ship could not bear it; but the lieutenant replied, 'Damn me, sir, if you can manage the ship better than I can, you had better take the command.' Myself and a good many more were at the waist of the ship and at the gangways, and heard what passed, as we knew the danger, and began to feel aggrieved; for there were some capital seamen aboard, who knew what they were about quite as well or better than the officers.

The Narrative of the Loss of the Royal George at Spithead, 1782, Anon, 1845

Too late, the officer realised his mistake and ordered the ship righted. Water rushed in and she sank in minutes. At the time, sailors not realising their danger, saw mice swimming in the hold and were betting on the best swimmer. As she capsized, a newly commissioned Lieutenant on deck jumped overboard with the shout "It's all over, but I must try to save this coat." Others followed, and a few below decks managed to climb out of the port-holes as she sank. Those who couldn't swim grabbed those who could, dragging all to the seabed, some in groups of 30 or 40. One 12-year-old boy was saved by the ship's captain, who said to him: "Pierce, can you swim?" to which he replied, "No." "Then you must try," and threw him overboard. The boy caught hold of a seaman who could swim. After the whirlpool formed by the sinking ship dissipated, he was placed in the rigging which still protruded from the Solent after the ship settled.

The boy noted by Beatrix Potter who clung to a sheep was rescued and later adopted by a wherryman. Not knowing his mother or father's name, only that he was called Jack, he was christened John Lamb. His story inspired a nautical drama on his supposed parentage and adventures, which toured the country to great success.

An estimated 1200 people were aboard, including women and children. Approximately 900 drowned; around 300 were women and 60 were children. Of the original 1200, only 255 survived. Bodies washed up along the Solent shores for weeks. The subsequent inquiry downplayed the actions of the lieutenant, who drowned with so many others, blaming the catastrophe on the wind and the state of the ship's timbers, which it was alleged, were rotten. Many were aggrieved at the Admiralty's denial of responsibility.

The story has an unexpected footnote. The wreck was a danger to shipping, and so -

Various attempts were made to remove it, but with very slight success, until in the year 1859 Colonel Pasley, a Royal Engineer officer, undertook the work, with a detachment of his corps, and in the course of six seasons effected its entire demolition and removal. Some of the guns had been already recovered; but those still at the bottom were valued at more than £5000. Professional divers were employed for a short time, but afterwards sappers were trained to the work, and their experiences under the water were not a little curious. On on occasion a pair of rival divers encountered at the bottom of the sea, having both seized the same piece of wreck timber. A scuffle ensued, in which "Corporal Jones" kicked out the eye or lens of "Private Girwan's" helmet, who would of course have been drowned had he not been instantly hauled to the surface.

A Handbook For Travellers In Surrey, Hampshire
And The Isle Of Wight – 1876

The timber recovered from the wreck was sold. I once had in my possession a small book called *The Narrative of the Loss of the Royal George*. It had curious highly polished wooden covers, made from the timber raised from the wreck.

Thus the buoy that Beatrix Potter saw on the Solent during her stay at the Queen's Hotel.

Now, perhaps we should move on to something more cheery?

26 Clarence Pier

Picture 31: Clarence Pier, drawing, c. 1890

Let's walk from the Queen's Hotel across the Common towards the structure that looks like it might hide one of the Thunderbirds: the modernday Clarence Pier. Its predecessor is pictured in the full-page drawing opposite.

It was named after the Duke of FitzClarence, who had the promenade built while he was town governor. The buildings to the right of the pier in the picture were the King's Assembly Rooms, with private and public baths for ladies and gentlemen, a laundry, living room, billiard room and engineer's living quarters with bedroom. Besides a large brick chimney, the rest was of light construction to enable quick removal in case of invasion. The Assembly Rooms and baths were opened in 1871 and the pier followed in 1882, opened by the Prince and Princess of Wales, with music supplied by the combined bands of the Royal Marine Artillery and Royal Marine Light Infantry. It soon became a centre for entertainment.

'That's Southsea, where the pier is. We used to go out there on Sundays on the bus, and go swimming. It's good – there's a boating lake and rock gardens, and a fair at Clarence Pier, see?'

A Girl Called Thursday, Lilian Harry, 2002

The simple pleasures of Southsea were captured by another writer in the 1920s, Clement Scott:

But a short detour takes me to the very end of the Southsea embankment, and then my course is straight, briny, and breezy, right away to the Clarence Pier, where all day long, with never-ending interest, they watch the steamers going to and returning from the Isle of Wight; they delight in the white-winged yachts that skim in and out of Portsmouth Harbour; they talk, and smoke, and eat chocolate, and flirt; they invest innumerable pence on the automatic boxes...

But there is something more to be seen on the Clarence Pier, afternoon and evening, than the harmless nonsense of the seaside. Here come popular artists from London to sing at first-class concerts, and here may be heard the magnificent strong band of the Royal Marine Artillery. In fact, Southsea boasts two piers, one at the Eastney end, and one at the Portsmouth end, and both piers are devoted to good music and automatic machines. Between the piers is a kind of mutual Campo Santo, facing the sea, where they erect monuments, tombstones, and cenotaphs to distinguished men beloved of Southsea and its immediate district. It is a strange fancy to mix up boats and bathing-machines, restaurants and lollypops, with seaside tombstones and granite memorials; but I do not think it is an inappropriate place for such humble and affectionate memorials of good men and great deeds of the deep.

Municipally considered, I don't suppose that there are two smarter sea-coast places in the south than Southsea and Portsmouth. Everything for the public service, such as cabs and lighting and good roads and order, is admirably managed at both places; but I very much doubt if "old salts" would recognise the Portsmouth of Charles Dickens and Captain Marryat... in the new, smart, red-bricked Portsmouth, with its magnificent barracks, park, and recreation ground, its imposing town hall – one of the finest in the kingdom – in the Portsmouth up-to-date, which only requires a new railway station to make it perfect.

Sisters by the Sea, Clement Scott, 1897

It's true that the memory of war is ever present in Southsea. Local author and aerospace engineer Nevil Shute uses the pier for dark and dramatic effect in the blackout.

The dance-hall was built out upon a pier on the seafront. Beneath their feet the tide crept in over the sand, menacing in the utter darkness. Outside no lights whatever showed upon the waste of waters. On the black, tumbling sea a very few ships moved unseen, unlit, and stealthily.

Landfall, Nevil Shute, 1940

Shute's description places the frivolous alongside the serious and dangerous. This motif is true for Portsmouth, which is both a seaside resort and the home of the fleet. It's a city of contrasts and contradictions.

I have fond memories of Clarence Pier. I used to catch the bus here as a boy with my older brother when he visited from London. He had the sweetest tooth, and would buy stacks of Mars bars and Twixes, and then share them selflessly. We would play on the arcade games and eat sweets all day long, then drink tea and gobble fish and chips by the water.

It was the simplest fun you could have and the most honest, and we would catch the bus home and sleep with sugar in our veins, battered cod in our tummies and happy dreams in our heads.

SOUTHSEA PIER.

27 Clarence Pier, on the deck

Picture 32: Clarence Pier from the beach, postcard, 1910
Picture 33: Clarence Pier on the deck, postcard, 1904

Let's step on to Clarence Pier. It's a very different structure from the one in the picture. Heavily damaged in World War 2, it was rebuilt in concrete. The pictures show the pier as it was when it was a landing stage for paddlesteamers and pleasureboats. A similar scene would have met Arthur Conan Doyle's eyes when he first set foot on the island of Portsea, a moment well worth celebrating.

One fine day towards the end of June in the year 1882 a young man stepped ashore from a coastal steamer at Clarence Pier, at the western and of Southsea Common. He was tall, broad-shouldered, with plump cheeks, a well-developed moustache and a pair of sharp, bold eyes which hinted that although it was only a month after his twenty-third birthday he had already been around a bit and could look after himself nicely, thank you. He was dressed in comfortable tweeds, complete with waistcoat and stiff collar and ties despite the time of year. With him he had all his worldly possessions: a tin box containing his top hat (every respectable Victorian gentleman with any pretensions to professional respctability had to have a top-hat, and consequently a box to carry it in) and a leather trunk. It must have been a pretty heavy trunk, because not only did it contain his best suit, spare pair of boots (shoes were not commonly worn by men, being considered effeminate), linen and toilet things and a few essential books, but also a brass plate inscribed with his name and medical degree, and his photographic gear, comprising at least a large wooden box camera, separate lens, and a set of glass photographic plates. Young Doctor Conan Doyle had arrived to seek his fortune as a general practitioner in Portsmouth.

A Study In Southsea, Geoffrey Stavert. 1987

As he stood here, he couldn't have known that this was the start of a period that would bring him so much success. Doyle would marry in Portsmouth, dabble in the paranormal, declare himself a Spiritualist - and create the world's greatest consulting detective, Sherlock Holmes. Portsmouth, it turned out, would suit Conan Doyle very well. For him it would be a land of opportunity.

Now, to the beach, just along the promenade.

On Clarence Pier, Southsea.

28 Clarence Beach

⁀

Picture 34: Clarence Beach postcard, 1900s
Picture 35: Southsea Beach, engraving from the Illustrated London News, 1882

Walking by the water in the 18th Century, you might have encountered an eccentric figure, Portsmouth native Jonas Hanway. Born in 1712, Hanway is best remembered for his introduction of the umbrella to Britain from Portugal and his first book, a true account of his misfortunes and adventures with pirates and brigands as he made his way across Russia in 1743 after a disastrous attempt to evaluate a new trade route to Persia. *An Historical Account of the British Trade Over The Caspian Sea* (1754) made him famous. His next book, the slightly less ambitious *A Journal of Eight Days Journey from Portsmouth to Kingston Upon Thames,* led the great literary critic Samuel Johnson to claim that Hanway had "acquired some reputation by travelling abroad, but lost it all by travelling at home." That second book begins:

Portsmouth had been now, for many months, the rendezvous of the fashionable world; every gay young man of fortune, and woman also, in their circle of joyous amusements, took a transient view of it; whilst those who have a relish of one of the noblest sights, which art or industry has yet produced, considered our fleet of capital ships, at this time in particular, with delight and exultation. I was in search of health, but I enjoyed much pleasure also, on the water, in the good company of lively sea warriors, distinguished for their good sense as well as good nature.

A Journal of Eight Days Journey from Portsmouth to Kingston Upon Thames, Jonas Hanway, 1756

Even in 1756, we can see the idea of seabathing becoming fashionable. Writing in 1817, young local historian Lake Allen coloured his observations of Southsea's charms with local pride, and also with a premonition of future rivalries:

There is also a safe place for open bathing along the Southsea beach, where the sea covers a fine gravelly bottom to the length of half a mile. There are also convenient bathing machines fitted up and ranged along the shore; as the company which have for late years frequented Southampton are rapidly diminishing, we may naturally conclude that sea bathing at Portsmouth will increase in proportion; indeed, it is rather a matter of surprise that Southampton should ever have had the preference in this respect to Portsmouth, for surely when the

Clarence Beach, Southsea

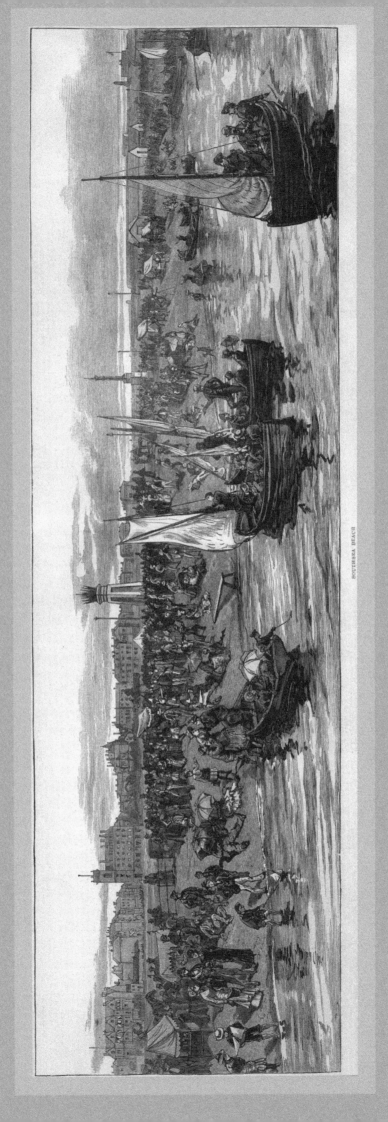

SOUTHSEA BEACH

shores are laved by the sea in all its saline strength, it must be preferable to a place like Southampton, where it is mixed with fresh water and by this means considerably weakened in its salutary effects on such as bathe for the recovery of their health, strength, or spirits.

The History of Portsmouth, Lake Allen, 1817

The postcard and print of the beach capture the resort in full swing. The engraving, with its crowds, pleasure boats and wherries, reminds me of Sir Walter Besant's writings:

We took our sculls and sails from the shop, and rigged our craft. She was built something on the lines of a wherry, for sea-worthiness, a strong, serviceable boat, not too heavy for a pair of sculls, and not too light to sail under good press of canvas. Everybody knew us on the beach—the boatmen, the old sailors, and the sailors' wives who were out with the children because the weather was so fine, all had a word to say to the Captain, touching their forelocks by way of preface. One carried our oars, another launched the boat, another sent a boy for a couple of rough sea-rugs, because the wind was high and the young lady might get wet, and in the midst of the general excitement we jumped in, and pushed off.

By Celia's Arbour, Walter Besant and James Rice, 1878

Of course, the beach was and is great for swimming...

Before us the waves ran along the shingle with a murmurous *sh—sh—sh*, or, if the day was rough, rolled up their hollow threatening crests like the upper teeth of a hungry monster's jaw, and then dashed in rage upon the stones, dragging them down with a crash and a roar which rolled unceasingly along the beach. In the summer months it was Leonard's delight at such times to strip and plunge, to swim over and through the great waves, riding to meet them, battling and wrestling till he grew tired, and came out red all over, and glowing with the exercise.

By Celia's Arbour, Walter Besant and James Rice, 1878

It wasn't only humans who swam, either. When the circus came to town, you'd catch the most unexpected of sights...

I blinked at the shoreline ahead, unable to credit my eyes.

Two sea-monsters were emerging from the waves. They squirted playful jets of water over the fearless man who led them ashore.

'Sanger's Circus,' Molly grinned. The red and white marquees dotted Southsea Common. 'Elephants' bath time.'

Lawless And The Three Pompey Piglets, from Portsmouth Fairy Tales for Grown-Ups, William Sutton, 2015

The modernday beach in Pauline Rowson's detective novels is similar in many ways (minus the elephants), though you never know if there's a body lurking round the corner.

Horton decided to follow suit soon afterwards, noting that Bliss had already left. As he headed along the busy promenade towards the marina where he lived on his yacht, he wasn't surprised to see that the pebbled beach was still packed with sunbathers. It was glorious cloudless evening, still hot but not with the intensity of the earlier heat of the day, and he toyed with the idea of getting a couple of hours' sailing in before sunset. He might have done except there was hardly a breath of wind. Instead, he sat on deck, enjoying the quiet of the evening and watching the sun set, trying to shut out thoughts of Woodley and work.

Death Lies Beneath, Pauline Rowson, 2012

Thankfully, no dead body this time. But I know Pauline Rowson's Inspector Andy Horton finds one somewhere along here, in one of her gripping stories.

29 Southsea Castle

Picture 36: Southsea Castle, engraving, c. 1830s
Picture 37: Southsea Castle, engraving, 1785

Let's follow Horton east, along the Promenade.

Keeping the sea on our right, we pass the hovercraft terminal and the Victory Anchor. Somewhere near here used to stand a monument to the gibbet from which the body of John Felton was hung in chains as a warning to others. Thankfully, the hanging of villains' bodies on the beach was discontinued some time ago, since it attracts a wholly different sort of tourist. :)

Thus we carry on along the promenade, passing the massive Lutyens-designed war memorial on the Common and, further on, Palmerston's Forts out in the sea on our right. A lovely description of the visual effect of this promenade from the Common was written by novelist Alison Habens:

No. 601.

Southsea Castle.

J. S. & Co.

They lived in a seaside town, where vast expanses of water, sky and shingle met in a single line. This was a horizon you could walk on, a promenade bustling in summer and bleak in winter. Half a mile of marshy grass lay between it and the shopping centre.

Lifestory, Alison Habens, 2003

Thus we reach, on our right hand side, Southsea Castle. People like to say that Henry VIII *built it,* but I suspect he didn't have the time to mix mortar and lay bricks, what with all that divorcing and beheading, arguing with the Pope and writing *Greensleeves* he was up to. He certainly *commissioned* the castle, and it was from here that he watched the tragic sinking of the Mary Rose, as Charles Kingsley relates:

And the king he screeched right out like any maid, 'Oh my gentlemen, oh my gallant men!

Westward Ho!, Charles Kingsley, 1855

Of course, castles are exactly the sorts of places where excitement must happen in novels. In the English Civil War, Parliamentary forces besieged it and children's adventure writer Percy F Westerman couldn't resist, describing his boy hero Humphrey Markham escaping the siege.

Cutting loose our steeds, we mounted, and, with sword and pistol, rode slowly towards the gateway. Here the sergeant unbarred the door and threw it suddenly open, and before the rebels, who were making for the gateway, were aware of our intention, the drawbridge had fallen with a run, and the four riders were urging their horses through the dense mass of men.

Taken by surprise, the musketeers, their pieces discharged and unloaded, gave way right and left, and, although a few pikemen amongst them tried to bar our way, our weight was irresistible.

I have a dim recollection of shearing off the head of an opposing pike, and seeing its holder's terror-stricken eyes, as he went down beneath my horse's hoofs. There was a crackle of pistol-shots, a flashing of steel, and we were through, tearing madly across the broad expanse of common on our bid for safety!

The Young Cavalier, Percy F Westerman, 1911

Early engravings show that the castle was remodelled in later years - but it was also remodelled by accident:

On August the 23rd, 1759, about eight o'clock in the morning, part of this Castle was blown up, by which many lives were lost: the particulars of this unfortunate accident are as follows:

The regiment, commanded by the Duke of Richmond, being encamped on Southsea Common, near the Castle, had permission given them to deposit their

Southsea Castle, 1785

powder and ball in the east wing of it. The day before the accident they had been filling cartridges for the exercise of the men, of which they had filled nine barrels, with the ball at the bottom of the barrels; these were placed in a lower room, over which there was a barrack where two women were washing and dressing victuals with a large fire of furze.

The flooring of the room being very old, it is supposed that some of the sparks of fire fell through the crevices of the floor on the loose powder the soldiers had carelessly scattered about in their work the day before, and communicated to the barrels, when in an instant, all that quarter of the Castle was blown up with a great explosion, and many people buried under the ruins.

One invalid soldier was blown out of the Castle, above an hundred yards, upon the glacis. He was much blackened by the powder and received a bruise on the head; the sentinel, another invalid, was blown over the parapet wall into the dry ditch, one leg and one arm being torn off, which were afterwards found lying on the parapet wall: it is remarkable that one man, as he stood on the wall, some little distance from the fatal spot, escaped without any other hurt than that the instant the explosion happened he was deprived of his senses, and remained for some time in the same position he was in when the event occurred; nor did he stir until being shaken by some people who saw him; he awaked as out of a sleep, without any recollection of what had happened.

There were seventeen men, women and children dug out of the rubbish, all dead except one old soldier, who breathed hard three or four times, and then expired.

The force of the explosion burst open the door of the large magazine to the west quarter of the Castle, where was lodged a great quantity of powder, and tore a large bolt off, but happily it reached no further; all the windows of the Castle were broken, and great part of the whole building damaged; the grand batteries towards the sea were not in the least affected, nor were any of those round the Castle, except in one place a little of the parapet wall towards the land was removed and the top of the wall thrown down.

A History of Portsmouth, Lake Allen, 1817

A dreamier description comes from Walter Besant, with a little more information about its history:

In those days the new suburb, which is now a large town, had hardly yet begun; there was no sea-wall along the beach outside the harbour, and half a mile beyond the rampart you might reach a place perfectly lonely and deserted. There was a common, a strip of waste land where the troops drilled and exercised, and beyond the common an old castle, a square and rather ugly pile built by Henry VIII., when he set up the fortresses of Sandown, Walmer, and Deal. It was surrounded by a star fort, and stood on the very edge of the sea, with a sloping face of stone which ran down to the edge of the water at low tide, and into the waves at high, protecting the moat which surrounded the town. As a boy I regarded this fortress with reverence. There had been a siege there at the time of the Civil War. It was held for the King, but the governor, after a little fighting with his Roundhead besiegers, surrendered the castle, and then the town itself capitulated. One pictured the townsmen on the wall, looking out to see the fortunes of the battle, the men for Church and King side by side with their sour-faced brethren who were for God and country, the discomfiture of the former when the Royal Standard was hauled down, and the joy of the Puritans when their party marched in at the town gates. Of course in my young imagination I supposed that the town walls were just the same then as now, with their bastions, curtains, ravelins, and glacis. It was a lonely place in those days, fit for a dreamy boy, or a moody man.

By Celia's Arbour, Sir Walter Besant and James Rice, 1878

Rather than a desolate and wild space, the area around the castle nowadays has fortified earthworks on either side, the Pyramids Centre, with its swimming pools and saunas, and the Rock Gardens to the east. The town walls, formerly in the distance, are long gone. A hint of what they were like can be seen just near to the garrison church we passed earlier. It's probably a good thing they're gone – those walls dominated Portsmouth, making it damp dark and squalid – very different from Southsea, with its sky arching over the sea and the wide open common nearby.

Southsea Castle, 1797

30 The Ladies' Mile

༄

Picture 38: The Ladies Mile, postcard, c.1914
Picture 39: The Ladies Mile, postcard, c.1930

Whilst we are in the vicinity of Southsea Castle, let's visit The Ladies Mile – a path across Southsea Common not far from Southsea Castle and the bottom of Palmerston Road.

You can get to it by walking out from the gate of Southsea Castle, past the D-Day Museum on your left, and up the Avenue De Caen.

The Ladies Mile is lined with trees, including some of the few mature elms left in Britain after they were decimated by Dutch Elm Disease. Here in the 19th Century the ladies of the town would promenade in their finery and perhaps smile and flirt with their beaux.

Before Southsea became a resort, the ground of the common comprised shingle beach, marshland, furze bushes and a great morass that was permanently flooded. At one entrance stood an arch made of the jawbones of a whale. It was a bleak site.

Walter Besant describes some of the lonely feel of the place before drainage and civilization arrived:

Sometimes, too, we would find gipsy encampments planted among the furze, with their gaudily-painted carts, their black tents—every real Romany has a black tent like the modern Bedawi or the ancient dweller in the tents of Kedar. While we looked at the bright-eyed children and the marvellous old women crouching over the fire of sticks and the great black pot, there would come out of the tents one or two girls with olive skins and almond eyes—not the almond eyes of Syria, but bolder, darker, and brighter. They would come smiling in Leonard's face, asking him to cross his hand with silver. When he said he had no silver they would tell his fortune for nothing, reading the lines of his palm with a glibness which showed their knowledge of the art. But it was always a beautiful fortune, with love, fighting, wife, and children in it.

By Celia's Arbour, Walter Besant and James Rice, 1878

The exotic flavour that Besant brings to the description is a masterpiece in childhood wonder, but Southsea Common has also been used for stranger and darker stories.

Such is the case with the strangely muted scene we experience below, as Meg and her dog Spencer lose their way in the mist in an eerie encounter with something strange and ghostly.

It was all right to start with. The mist was worse than ever but we had made a joint decision not to go further than a quick trot round the common that leads down to the sea. It was deserted, which wasn't surprising, given the weather and the time. There was a silence and a stillness that was unusual. I know it sounds odd but I remember that I found it strangely moving. The place looked eerily beautiful and for a while I was happy for Spencer and I to have it to ourselves. The tops of the trees were just about visible, like black lace emerging from a white fur cloak. I could see the lights from the street lamps glowing in the distance like eyes. But as we went on, the mist seemed to sink until it surrounded us completely, just as it had on the beach earlier. Spencer usually runs round a bit but not that night. He stuck by my side, determined for us not be separated. And he was right. For the second time we heard a noise but this was different. It was not the beating of wings, it was hooves...

Heads and Tails, in Portsmouth Fairy Tales for Grown-Ups, Diana Bretherick, 2015

And so, we come to the final of the many reasons for the nickname *Pompey*. This one is that in the 18th Century, volunteer firemen, who were known as *pompiers* (from the French for *pumpmen*) exercised on Southsea Common.

True or not, the place we are going next could have done with some pompiers nearby, at least twice in the last century.

The Ladies Mile, 1910s..

The Ladies Mile, Southsea.

THE LADIES MILE, SOUTHSEA

218156

...and in the 1930s.

31 South Parade Pier

Picture 40: South Parade Pier drawing, 1890s
Picture 41: South Parade Pier, postcard 1910s
Picture 42: South Parade Pier, postcard, 1930s

Let's head along the Ladies Mile, cross Cockrill Way (named after Jack Cockrill, the inventor of the hovercraft) then cross the road on your right to arrive back at the seafront, just east of the Rock Gardens. Here, in *The Restless Tide,* Julia Bryant describes her characters "weaving in and out of the groups of sailors and holidaymakers" and passing a preacher on Speakers' Corner "haranguing anyone willing to stop and listen." These days, it's rare to see anyone sermonising here, but there are plenty of skateboarders on summer evenings and you find performers here sometimes in the summer, entertaining passers-by.

Further along the seafront we come to South Parade Pier. The large picture of the pier opposite dates from the 1890s. This small, elegant structure was built in 1879 and burned down in 1904. The next incarnation was a far more glamorous affair, with a galleried theatre for top notch entertainments, and in the 1950s there were fireworks at the end of the pier regularly in the summer. The place was alive with the bustle of holidaymakers.

Here's the council's description of the seaside resort from that period.

The magnificent stretch of the Southsea coastline is an enchanted place of colour, gaiety and sparkle, where a thousand and one delights attract the seeker after health and enjoyment.

The South Parade Pier is the mecca of entertainment. A magnificent theatre stages ideal summer attractions, and in the Minor Hall light refreshments are served to the accompaniment of a modern Hammond Organ. On the Pier Deck, an orchestra plays daily, interspersed with Gala evening and firework displays. From the Pierhead steamers ply daily to the Isle of Wight and launches depart frequently throughout the day for trips around Portsmouth Harbour. There is never a dull moment. It is not surprising that this happiest of resorts, beloved by millions, grows in popularity by leaps and bounds.

Portsmouth and Southsea Official Guide, c.1956

This upbeat description makes for excellent copywriting in its own right, but Portsmouth writers have a tendency to turn the upbeat over, and find the dark shadow it is casting underneath. Such is the case with Neil Gaiman's early graphic Novel, *Mr Punch,* though at this stage the real darkness of the work is not yet fully apparent:

In the summer holidays I would usually be sent to stay with my maternal grandparents, at the seaside. My grandparents, Ruby and Arthur, lived in a house too large for them in Southsea; there were three locked rooms on the top floor, and the knowledge of their existence always coloured my stays there.

Another vivid memory: six years old, a performance of Toad of Toad Hall on the sea-front. It was a burning summer's day. The performance spoiled me for any other, for the actors performed in full-body costumes, accurate in every detail: the Badger, the Mole, the Rat, the Toad, the Weasels and Ferrets and Stoats, huge animals that danced and joked and sang on the stage just for me, although my memories of the story and songs are cloudy at best.

The Tragical Comedy And Comical Tragedy Of Mr Punch,
Neil Gaiman, 1994

Jonathan Meades uses the pier for his broad cracked humour in his extreme and at times shocking novel *Pompey:*

I rented this booth on the pier. Between Madame Phillipina the fortune teller and the live bait. She was a bigamist ten times over, smoked roll-ups, must have been seventy. She used to go down the end to the landing stage and tell me what she'd seen over on Ryde Pier. She believed it. Courting couple in identical anoraks; man throwing sackful of cats into the briny (she always said 'briny'). This is four, five miles away. She could see through time and distance, she said...

She'd get people coming back and complaining. There was this old bloke who'd given up the lease on his beach hut because she'd told him he was going to die in the winter – next summer came round, and there he was, fit as a fiddle but with nowhere to change into his cozzie. She'd made him believe *that,* that he was going to throw a seven; it's not what anyone *wants* to believe is it? She was that convincing.

Pompey, Jonathan Meades, 1993

The pier burned down again in 1974 during the shooting of the film *Tommy.* It was a disaster for the city at the time,

but for one Pompey resident who was a film extra decked out in designer clothing from Chanel it was a blessing. She got to keep the jewellery and dress she was wearing. "No one was interested in my giving it back," she told me. "It all got claimed on the insurance."

Modern Portsmouth writers being what they are, the darker side of the town often comes though. This is just the case in the way Pauline Rowson uses the pier in the following scene set outside the nightclubs that used to stand opposite the pier. It feels very authentic.

Outside Horton breathed in the night air hoping to banish his acute sensation of isolation, but the fog was as suffocating as ever. He climbed on his Harley and rode home carefully and slowly. His route took him along the mist-shrouded seafront where the sound of the booming foghorns filled the air. There were young people milling around outside the nightclubs, and a police wagon was parked in front of the pier. Later, when club land spewed its contents on to the pavements, there would be drunken young people and scantily clad girls everywhere. He wondered if this would be Emma's fate. God, he hoped not. He wanted to play a part in her upbringing, and he knew deep in his heart that it had to be more than just a once-a-week visit.

The Suffocating Sea, Pauline Rowson, 2008

I used to go to those nightclubs. The original Savoy Ballrooms through whose windows summer light filtered into an elegant dance room in the 1950s had altered over the years to become, by my time in the 1980s, a string of sweaty nightclubs deafening and dazzling, where fights broke out over taxis and lovers at closing time.

My memories of clubland include a girl I met who told me how she came out from the club one hot summer's night, stripped off and stepped into the sea.

"I just wanted to float away," she told me. "I closed my eyes and lay back in the water and let the tide take me."

The RNLI picked her up from the water about two hours later. She was still drunk and fought with them when they tried to take her on board.

The pier has had a long and varied history. I've included in the pictures two postcards showing how it was before its current incarnation, one from the side in the 1910s and another from the 1930s taken from outside the old Savoy Ballrooms, with a row of cars parked along the front.

And who says the parking problem in Southsea is new?

SOUTH PARADE PIER
SOUTHSEA

South Parade Pier, Southsea.

32 Romantic Southsea

Picture 43: What The Moon Saw At Southsea, Postcard, c.1918
Picture 44: Southsea, too busy to write, c.1910

Since we are talking about the sea, holidays and leisure, we naturally come to the matter of love. These two postcards capture beautifully one of the great subjects that advertisers for the town sought to promote – the holiday romance.

And yes, it really is a romantic scene as we walk along the beach, continuing east - although I'll be honest, the sand in the picture is a little *too* romantic. You'll find pebbles here, more often than sand.

For some reason, romance tends to be far from the minds of most writers about Portsmouth. There are a few notable exceptions, including, of course, Jane Austen. Since her brothers were naval officers, she was often in Portsmouth, travelling down from her small house at Chawton deep in the Hampshire countryside to visit. Austen uses the seafront to great effect for her heroine, Fanny Price:

The day was uncommonly lovely. It was really March; but it was April in its mild air, brisk soft wind, and bright sun, occasionally clouded for a minute; and everything looked so beautiful under the influence of such a sky, the effects of the shadows pursuing each other on the ships at Spithead and the island beyond, with the ever-varying hues of the sea, now at high water, dancing in its glee and dashing against the ramparts with so fine a sound, produced altogether such a combination of charms for Fanny, as made her gradually almost careless of the circumstances under which she felt them. Nay, had she been without his arm, she would soon have known that she needed it, for she wanted strength for a two hours' saunter of this kind, coming, as it generally did, upon a week's previous inactivity. Fanny was beginning to feel the effect of being debarred from her usual regular exercise; she had lost ground as to health since her being in Portsmouth; and but for Mr. Crawford and the beauty of the weather would soon have been knocked up now.

Mansfield Park, Jane Austen, 1814

A modern romance writer who set her work in Regency Portsmouth is Scottish author M C Beaton, whose "Travelling Matchmaker" series sees various heroines visit alliterative cities only to find true love. *Penelope Goes to Portsmouth* is the perfect book to read on the beach in Southsea if you're looking for pulp romance. Here's a little flavour of it, toward its denouement:

'You will marry me, will you not?'

'Oh, yes,' said Penelope, her heart in her eyes.

Oblivious of the watching guests, the dripping-wet lord pulled her back into his arms and kissed her soundly. Several cheered...

Penelope Goes To Portsmouth, M C Beaton, 1991

Why the Lord in question was dripping wet, how her heart got to be "in her eyes" and why people cheered... Well, you'd have to read it to find out.

SOUTHSEA.

Too busy to write.

33 Southsea Pebbles

Picture 42: *Old Rooster Little Duck postcard, c. 1930s*
Picture 43: *Pebbles On The Beach, postcard, c. 1910*
Picture 44: *Woman In A Barrel, postcard, c.1920s*

From romance to fun, with three postcards: the finder of "a pebble" on the beach, a "young hen" and a nude woman in a barrel. They're classic seaside postcards.

The card opposite, with its mention of pebbles reminded me of Graham Hurley's character Gillespie, his experience with pebbles, and how a routine day begins to hint at the serious situation to come:

He set off down the street, running slowly at first, his breath clouding on the cold air, his arms and legs moving sweetly under the cotton flannel of his ancient tracksuit. He ran every morning at dawn, seven days a week. He'd done it since he could remember, since he first joined the Corps, and it had become part of his life. He pushed himself to the limit, running the length of the city's beach, five hard miles of pebbles, winter and summer. The pebbles drained the strength from his legs, but the feeling it gave him at the end, when he stopped to recover, was quite irreplaceable. It meant that nothing during the next twenty-four hours could touch him. It made him feel somehow immortal, beyond danger, beyond compromise, beyond reach...

...On the seafront he paused. A convoy of Army lorries swept past him. There were squaddies in combat gear squatting on the slatted wooden benches in the backs of the trucks. Their faces were daubed with camouflage cream, and they cradled SA80 assault rifles in their laps. They wore black berets low over their eyes, gazing at him with the kind of watchful indifference he remembered so well from Berlin.

Rules of Engagement, Graham Hurley, 1990

For Portsmouth writers, the strange is never far off... thus Diana Bretherick reveals the sinister side of pebbles:

I remember it so clearly. It was one of those strange days in early spring when the sun shines as if it's summer but the air is still cold. Meg decided to venture onto Southsea beach as part of our early morning walk. She sat and squinted, looking out to sea as I snuffled about in my usual way, more to fulfil expectations rather than anything else. Then I found them – three stones staring at me with those deep black eyes. I stared back; a mistake, as it turned out. They responded by...well, I know it sounds ridiculous – by biting me. I yelped in shock and pain. Meg came running over.

Heads and Tails, in Portsmouth Fairy Tales for Grown-Ups, Diana Bretherick, 2015

There's trouble when an old rooster falls in love with a little duck at SOUTHSEA.

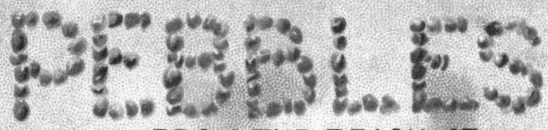

PEBBLES

FROM THE BEACH AT

SOUTHSEA.

I found such a lovely little Pebble on the Beach, to-day, at Southsea.

I'm going to keep it.

Other artists and writers have used the pebbles in other ways. Portsmouth-based artist Pete Codling ran a project to create a million handmade pebbles between 1994 and 2011. 300,000 community members joined in, and the pebbles were placed on Southsea beach.

Another writer, poet Katie Gill writes:

These pebbles glisten with the tears of the Blitz,
are ragged and misshapen with the footprints
of soldiers marching towards the D-Day landings,
Pick one up and examine it.
You'll see the scars of a resilient yet underrated city,
one that was once the most fortified in Europe,
so before you turn your nose up,
know that this is the Philip Pirrip of towns
because we've got Great Expectations -
we may be small and unassuming, but we're
irrepressible.

from Pompey 'Til I Die, by Katie Gill, 2017

But from a fun romantic postcard about pebbles, this all now seems quite serious.

The woman in the barrel and the old rooster with his little hen are, I hope, antidotes to too much graveness!

34 Eastney Esplanade & Canoe Lake

Picture 47: Beach Parade and Canoe Lake

Let's carry on along the front a while longer. Now we come to "Beach Parade" (as it's called in the postcard), with Canoe Lake on the far side of the road, which, interestingly enough, is edged by a road called "The Ocean At The End of Lane", named after the novel by Neil Gaiman.

The picture I've used for this end of the beach dates from around 1918, and shows it full of bathing machines to protect the modesty of bathers, and allow them entry to the water without being watched by unwanted eyes – or, I have to add, having their feet nobbled (or even nibbled, if we take Diana Bretherick's former story as a guide) by all those pebbles.

In the background, you can see Canoe Lake, which is all that remains of the Great Morass, an area of marshland which covered much of the Common north and east of Southsea Castle. A map of 1716 shows it stretching up to fields on the far side of a track which maps on to the line of modernday Albert Road. To the east, a finger of water stretched to Lump's Fort, close to the Royal Marines Barracks.

By 1884, the wetland of the Great Morass was in a sorry state, described by one writer as "a dismal-looking depression, strewn with rusty tins, mouldy rubbish and other abominations."

Thus, the council took charge, drained the swamp and built the boating lake, upon which swan pedalos have been plying the water since the early part of the the 20th Century. What real swans think about this has not been ascertained.

I have been holding off using examples of my own writing to illustrate the area, but if you don't mind with this location I am going to break my rule. In my novel *The Snow Witch*, Canoe Lake and the surrounding area are central to the early action in the story. Here, we encounter Riley on an icy winter's night, where snow has been falling for days. It's a dark tale, and the writing is suitably sombre.

Beach, Parade, & Canoe Lake Southsea.

He arrives at a white expanse, the heads of black railings jut from the snow; nearby, a stunted litter bin: a dwarf sentry in white-domed helmet. In the middle distance, a ring of plastic swans – a lake, indistinct, as are the roads and garden edges around it.

Here he is: *back in time*; back here at the lake across from his mother's house.

On the water's surface he feels the crunch of snow, and the *crack* and *boom* as the ice sheet tenses. He heads with purpose to the plastic pedalos, relics of the '60s with swan necks and funny-grotesque faces. He climbs on and sprawls across them, letting his head go back, snowflakes melting on his upturned face and delivering remembrance:

From the window of my mother's house; kids playing; sparkling water. The old man in his flat cap palming coins and notes in return for twenty shimmering minutes; he's watching for me coz of that time I took a boat. To go where?

He sees himself: a directionless impulse surrounded by concrete banks; no escape except if that plastic swan should stretch its wings and fly. *No chance.*

The Snow Witch, Matt Wingett, 2017

Since I'm shamelessly using my own work, I must add: if you like what you've read, please go and buy at least one copy.

For all of your friends.

Each.

:)

The Snow Witch

Matt Wingett

35 The Solent Sky

❧

Picture 48: Schneider Trophy

A little way further along the front, we reach the former Royal Marines Barracks, with Lump's Fort next to it. The picture I've chosen is the programme cover for the final Schneider Trophy, that was won over the Solent in 1931.

French balloonist, aviationist and all round flight enthusiast Jacques Schneider created the seaplane speed trials in 1913 to promote excellence in aviation – his dream being that cheap flight would one day be available to all. Thus, between 1913 and 1931, competitions were arranged, the winning country hosting the next. If a country won three times in a row, they would claim the title forever. Thus, after winning in Venice in 1927, Britain hosted and won in 1929, and 1931 – both times on the Solent.

Newspapers estimated that a million people descended on the south coast for the weekend of the 1929 race. *The Evening News* reported that the perfect, still, bright weather conditions allowed all-night bathing parties on the moonlit beach, and added, "As dawn broke over Southsea beach to-day, armies of laughing girls lit fires and stoves all along the sands and began to cook breakfast. The fragrance of eggs and bacon spread for miles."

Britain's victory has a legendary status for aviationists. The designer of the winning British aircraft was R J Mitchell, who used lessons learned in Portsmouth to design the Spitfire. RAF officer T E Shaw also attended, and on seeing how slowly recovery boats got out to crashed aircraft recommended the RAF develop a fast boat service for Air Sea Rescue. One result of that recommendation was the World War 2 launch HSL102 which can be seen in the dockyard. Shaw was also known as T E Lawrence, or Lawrence of Arabia.

With all its naval associations, it is often forgotten that aviation was part of life in Portsmouth. There was an airport on the north-eastern side of Portsea Island, and Nevil Shute designed the first ever retractable aircraft undercarriage for the Airspeed Courier 5 that was built in Portsmouth. Shute lived at 14 Helena Road, Southsea, behind Canoe Lake. He featured Portsmouth in several of his novels. In *So Disdained*, a Soviet spyplane flies in past the Nab Tower off Southsea to take night-time photos of secret goings-on in the harbour:

'I throttled down at the Nab,' he said, 'and then we went creeping in, doing about eighty, and so quiet that I might have heard my watch ticking if I'd put it to my ear. I had the parachute flare all ready, with a little stick to poke it down the tube with. It was the entrance to the harbour that I had to take – the narrow part.'

So Disdained, Nevil Shute, 1928

But Shute wasn't the only author to use aircraft in adventures over Portsmouth. Percy F Westerman, the author of sci-fi fantasy *The Flying Submarine*, wrote of a super-fast airship in the skies over the island ciry in another novel in 1919:

"By Jove! We're passing Southampton Water," ejaculated Dacres. He again glanced at his watch. It had taken him three and a half minutes to traverse the length of the "Meteor," and in that space of time the airship had travelled eleven miles.

"Top speed now," announced Whittinghame. "We're doing one hundred and ninety. We'll have to slacken down now; we're nearly there."

As he spoke the Captain rang down for half speed. The order being simultaneously received by both engine-rooms, resulted in a gradual slowing down till the mud-flats of Portsmouth Harbour hove in sight. Even then the "Meteor" overhauled a naval seaplane as quickly as an express runs past a "suburban" crawling into Clapham Junction.

The Dreadnought of the Air, Percy F Westerman, 1914

I love the way futuristic writers clunkily use the technology they know to predict the future.

But aircraft weren't the stuff of fantasy. Pleasure flights took off from the Common in the 1920s – a normal occurrence after World War I, when numerous planes had been decommissioned, and demobbed pilots were looking for work. The plight of one such pilot selling pleasure flights on the south coast is central to Shute's *So Disdained*.

I wrote in the introduction about my 90-year-old neighbour's enjoyment of the spectacle of the Schneider Trophy. She described how she stretched out on the grass among the buttercups on Lump's Fort, near the Royal Marines Barracks at Eastney and watched the planes zooming by all day. She was in a kind of detached happy bliss. Queen of her own castle, the crowds didn't bother her, and she spent the day marvelling at the scene as the super-fast aircraft roared through the air.

I envy her firsthand experience. When I was a kid and I heard Britain had won the Schneider Trophy all those years ago to become the "forever reigning top nation at making planes" (as I saw it), I swelled with pride. Back then, I hadn't

THE SCHNEIDER TROPHY
SEPT. 12TH CONTEST - 1931 -

THE ROYAL AERO CLUB
OFFICIAL
SOUVENIR PROGRAMME

Printed and Published by   GALE & POLDEN LTD., LONDON, ALDERSHOT & PORTSMOUTH.   6D.

worked out that even after the prize-giving, people carry on striving. I learned that lesson later.

We are now at the Eastney end of the seafront, with the road veering left as it reaches the Fraser Range at the Front's far end. The area features heavily in Nevil Shute's *Requiem For A Wren* and is described by modern-day comedy author Pete Adams thus:

> Jack had left this magically energetic and hypnotically intimidating wave action behind as his morning walk followed the paved promenade eastwards and now skirted the expansive and desolate beach at Eastney seafront. Sweeping tracts of shingle, interspersed with tufts of sward clinging desperately to some sort of purchase that enabled it to survive, symbolised the barrenness of this eastern Portsmouth coastal landscape. The grey, churning and turbulent sea was dramatically electrified by voluminous black and agitated cloud formations and tantalisingly distant lightning. Jack walked and mused, he liked the barrenness, the lonely landscape that he often likened to his soul. There was nobody else in view, just Snail beside Jack's pastel marker beacon, a lemon beach hut in the distance.
>
> *Ghost and Ragman Roll, Pete Adams, 2017*

This brings us to the end of the Southsea leg of our tour. If you have walked the length of the seafront following this literary meander, well, I salute you. I do this walk quite often, so I know it's a good distance.

However, if you are in a car or on bike - or if your legs are stout and up for the walk, there are two more spots I'd like to show you.

The first is the smithy, on the page opposite.

36 Milton Smithy

❧

Picture 49: The Old Smithy, Milton, postcard, circa 1900

Follow the promenade along to the end of the seafront and it loops back, passing north and west by Bransbury Park on your right. Eventually, you come to a set of traffic lights. Take a right up Milton Road and keep going until you come to the Milton Arms. Somewhere along Priory Crescent to your left is where this photograph was taken, between 1890 and 1910.

The scene is a country idyll. All that remains of the former Milton Farm that stood here is Milton Park, with an old barn at its heart. Another former farm building is now the Milton Arms Barn where cows don't low, but bands play.

The Smithy itself appears on old Ordnance Survey maps on the north side of Priory Crescent.

This image is a reminder that not all of Portsmouth was devoted to heavy industry, the navy, pubs, leisure or prostitution. There was farmland (Lake Allen noted proudly in the early 19th Century that Portsmouth produced the best broccoli in the kingdom!) and there were small Hampshire villages well into the age of photography. Of the industry on the other side of the island, and the other sort of blacksmithing, Dickens writes eloquently of a trip to a blacksmith in the dockyard:

> We now approached a building of glass and iron (one of the many results of the first Crystal Palace), but dark and sooty-looking - the Blacksmiths' Shop. This is a comparatively new affair, the old blacksmiths' shop having been "a ramshackle place," as the sailors say. Glad to hail an improvement, and having with pleasure seen traces of the newer discoveries in machinery in the departments already visited, we enter this Crystal Palace of the Cyclops. The ring of hammers, the glare of forges, the passing to and fro of swarthy figures, strike all together upon us as we enter this spacious and convenient place, and see red-hot iron being manipulated as readily as ribbons. From three to four hundred men are at work here, on the various iron-work used in ship-building and ships. Lofty and airy as it is, we are glad to find ourselves in the air again - air flavoured by the salt of the sea.
>
> *Portsmouth, Charles Dickens, 1859*

The Old Smithy, Milton Portsmouth.

JWS 1162

But here, in Milton, we are in a far distant, countrified place:

> Removed from noisy strife,
> See Milton's shores and rural scenes, where blends
> With wild and decorative scenery, the rich
> and cultured soil.
>
> *Island of Portsea, from A Metrical History of Portsmouth,*
> *Henry Slight, 1820*

For me, the Milton Arms Barn evokes a fond memory, also to do with the production of fumes other than those mentioned by Dickens.

When I was a teenager, I had a punk band called *The Dogmongers* (what a name!). Our drummer was always keen to make more of an impact, as drummers always are, and told us he wanted to try out a smoke bomb effect at our Milton Arms gig, held in The Barn at the back of the pub.

When the time came and he lit the fuse, the smoke was amazing. The audience looked on impressed. Then, there was more smoke. And then there was more. What our drummer hadn't told us was the smoke bomb was designed for battlefield theatricals. Within four seconds I couldn't see the audience. Within six seconds, I couldn't see my hand in front of my face. It was chaos. I remember a rectangle of light where the doorway had been, and silhouetted figures disappearing through it, coughing their guts up.

Eventually, the smoke began to clear and the landlady materialised in the doorway, hands on hips, absolutely furious. She gave off a fine volley of rage along the line of "what the hell do you think you're playing at?" though a little more picturesque than that. She finished her tirade with: "That's it. You're banned from this pub. You'll never play here again."

There was a stunned silence. Then, just as she turned to leave, a friend's voice chimed up from the smoke:

"Don't mind my mum, everyone. She's all right really."

The landlady stamped off, even more furious, accompanied by the sound of raucous laughter .

That night, I was so *impressed* by the gig that I left the money we took at the door on top of the car – and scattered notes and coins down the road outside St Mary's Hospital.

The moral to this tale?

I don't think there is one.

37 The Great Salterns

Picture 50, The Great Salterns Farm, Anon, 1851

Heading up the road from the Milton Arms Barn, let's make one final stop on our literary and pictorial tour of Portsmouth. At the lights, go right along Velder Avenue, which becomes the Eastern Road, skirting the island's east side.

Some way up, you'll come to Great Salterns House, a mansion on your right hand side, overlooking the sea. Now a pub and restaurant, it's our final stop.

In the mid 19th Century, this was a quiet deserted place, with a track coming in from Great Salterns Farm, pictured on the facing page. A few of the farm's outbuildings still stand along Burrfields Road, across the Eastern Road from here.

Great Salterns House, (aka Great Salterns Mansion) is the setting for Victorian novelist Sarah Doudney's *The Great Salterns*. She is the last of our novelists in the book.

Born in Portsea in 1841, she spent much of her life in Cosham, not only writing Christian novels, but also church hymns. Here is how the mansion appears in the opening to her book. It also gives a little of the area's history of sea-salt manufacture, which was used by the navy to preserve its rations:

> It was a March afternoon; a fresh breeze was blowing off the sea, sweeping across the grassy flats and marshes, and fluttering Kate Bradley's coarse dress, as she stood looking out over the water. The tide was high; one or two crazy old blunt-headed boats were rocking on the ripples; and the spring sunshine rested peacefully on the slopes of Portsdown Hill, showing the great white chasms of the chalk-pits. Still farther off, lay the fair heights of Sussex, faint and blue in the distance; nearer, and on the right hand, were the coasts of Havant and Hayling. The white wings of a gull gleamed like silver as the light touched them in its graceful flight...
>
> ...She was standing on the edge of the road, which was raised above high-water mark. The water came gurgling round the piles and sea-stained stones that had resisted its advances for many a year. A wilder

(The Great Salterns Farm, Anon, 1851, reproduced by kind permission of Portsmouth Museums and Records Service, Portsmouth City Council, All rights reserved)

or more desolate spot could scarcely be found; yet at one time it had been the scene of busy occupation. Years ago, when the great salterns were in working order, the place teemed with life and industry, for the works had given employment to a large number of hands. But they had long been abandoned; fragments of ruined boiling-houses and sheds were still standing among the coarse grass and reeds, and adding to the dreary aspect of the waste land.

The road, strongly built on piles, crossed a bridge, under which the water flowed into the creeks. Then, slightly winding, it led on to the iron gate of the large, lonely house that stood with its back to the sea, while its front windows commanded a view of the level country. It was a square white mansion, almost encircled by its lawn and shrubberies. The road swept completely round it, but the evergreens inside its ivied fence had grown thick and strong, and it was so well guarded by trees, that few glimpses of its lower storeys could be obtained.

The Great Salterns, Sarah Doudney, 1875

Looking at the snowbound scene in the picture, here is a description of the cottage the story's lowly Kate Bradley lives in. It brings home the harsh realities of life in this once-desolate place:

The wooden cottage, pleasant and picturesque enough in summer, was hardly a desirable abode in this bitter weather. Streams of snow water were apt to make their way through the chinks in its walls, when the tardy sun shone forth; keen blasts penetrated it at all points; and Hilda had seen Simeon vainly attempting to keep them out.

The Great Salterns, Sarah Doudney, 1875

Great Salterns Mansion sits on what was, in the 1600s, a large bay called Gatcombe Haven. Steadily filled in during the following centuries, first by the creation of the salterns, and later by deliberate infilling and dumping of rubbish, all that is left of the original haven is the golf course's lake - though if you look on the map to the rear of this book, you'll see its footprint in the lack of housing that roughly follows its former shores.

Its memory also survives in the name of Gatcombe House, mentioned in Henry Slight's series of poems about Portsmouth. In this extract, he notes that Gatcombe House was built on the site of Gatcombe Priory, a long-forgotten "Holy Pile" lost in the mists of memory.

He goes on to sing the praises of a naval hero of his day who lived there, Admiral Sir Roger Curtis (he fought alongside the same Admiral Lord Howe we met earlier at the Spithead Mutiny) who lived in the smart new Gatcombe House:

Gatcombe we ponder on thy vistas green,
Where hoar tradition speaks of Holy Pile
'Mid spacious forest of majestic oak,
Unnoticed in the history of the Isle:
Howe'er well suited to the minstrel's lay,
We disregard it. Yet must the Muse
Here pay her homage to thy worth
Illustrious Curtis! who in ardent fight
Long time maintained the glory of our name,
And ever did his duty.
from A Metrical History of Portsmouth, Henry Slight, 1820

Soon, it will be time to finish.

I wanted to bring you here because there are very, very few fictitious accounts of this side of the island. It's probably true to say that Sarah Doudney, a well-established Victorian writer of moral tales who came from Portsmouth, cornered the market (small as it was).

I mentioned previously that Doudney wrote hymns, and I have one more piece of information about this side of her for you.

Curiously, her most famous composition was *The Christian's Good Night*, which underwent a resurrection in the late 20th Century when it was sung *a capella* at the end of gigs by the hippy rock band *The Grateful Dead*.

Brunel, Dickens, Kipling, Manning... and Doudney..?

Well, she isn't one of the great names of history, but I admit, I always feel a frisson of pleasure when I discover how far the work of Portsmouth people has reached - and in the most unexpected of places!

End Note

And that is the end of the tour. Thank you for sticking with it. It's been a little bit eccentric, and filled with both light and dark. It's true that for many, Portsmouth is a Marmite city, and I have sympathy for those writers in the past who've struggled to come to terms with it. But for all its flaws, others have loved it.

Right now, Portsmouth has a crop of fantastic writers. Writing is a tough business and it is difficult to earn a living in an age of giveaways, pirating and an ever more centralised publishing industry focussed on finding the Next Big Thing at the expense of quieter voices. I encourage you to seek out local writers. Go to spoken word events, support your artists. After all, we create things not just for ourselves, but for you. There is a list of all the books and their writers mentioned in this tour in the next few pages.

I'm going to finish with a poem by local poet Maggie Sawkins, who won the Ted Hughes Award for New Work in Poetry in 2013. In many ways it sums up how many of us feel about the town these days. Maggie is Southsea-based, but I'm sure many across the city will recognise the sentiment of feeling at home this poem evokes.

All that's left is for me to thank you once again for joining me on this tour, and to wish you a safe journey home!

Things to Do Around Southsea
By Maggie Sawkins

Sit where Steve Tebb, Drainman of Portsmouth, sat,
watch the dancing sea. Reminisce the Wild Mouse,
the Wall of Death, Uncle Charlie's tattoos.
Get married for the third time. Launch a book of poems.
Drink champagne at The Queen's.
Go for a curry.

Watch Syd Little in Cinderella at The King's.
The Spinnaker Tower lit up for Christmas.
Love Albert Road!
Go for a curry.

Take Amber Leaf and Milky Ways to a friend in St James'.
Think about the man who stole a turkey from Tesco's.
Lend someone a score. Talk to seagulls. Play crazy golf.
Listen to the cursing sea.
Go for a curry.

Take a red geranium to Bett at St Vincent's,
watch Des O'Connor on plasma TV.
Fly a kite on the common.
Consider a swim.
Go for a curry.

Watch Red Arrows draw love hearts over South Parade Pier.
Buy okra and cardamoms from Akram's for later.
Put change into the Bangladeshi welfare tin.
Collect Robin from the hover. Inhale the sea.
Have a glass or three at The Phoenix.
Talk about times. Love Albert Road!
Go for a curry.

See Angelhart Quartet at The King Street Tavern.
Disgrace oneself in an Aqua taxi.
Sleep it off. Write a poem.
Go for a curry.

This poem by Maggie Sawkins from This Island City,
anthology, 2010

Works Mentioned In This Book

The books listed below all reference Portsmouth in some way. Some feature the town, others, such as Wodehouse's *Uneasy Money* give it a glancing mention. Yet I included Wodehouse because he lived only a few miles off the island in Emsworth, and so is included by virtue of proximity. The list is by no means exhaustive - indeed, I found more writers just as I finished writing this book – but this gives you a starting point from which to explore.

Please note, my focus has been primarily on novels. I should add that there is a vibrant and rich community of poets in Portsmouth. I have tried to include examples of some of their works, but Portsmouth Poetry is a whole book in itself. Indeed, *This Island City*, published by Spinnaker Press is that book, and I recommend it for poetry lovers.

There are in fact so many quality poets in Portsmouth that I think they might consider renaming the city *Poetsmouth*. What a typo will reveal!

Honourable mentions should also go to *The Portsmouth Papers*. I've added a list of ones that might interest the reader looking for more detailed information about Portsmouth. You can buy them from the City Musem and Libraries.

Books from Life Is Amazing

I have started republishing more scarce Portsmouth-related works. I am making these available from my website, at wwwlifeisamazing.co.uk post-free within the UK.

In the list below, those titles not yet published at time of writing are marked with an asterisk.

Books Featuring Portsmouth or Portsmouth Writers Available from Life Is Amazing

Fiction:
By Celia's Arbour, Walter Besant and James Rice
Charlotte Temple*, Susannah Haswell Rowson
Dark City, edited by Karl Bell and Stephen Pryde-Jarman
Day of the Dead, Anthology
A Metrical History of Portsmouth*, Henry Slight
Portsmouth Fairy Tales for Grown-Ups, Anthology
The Great Salterns*, Sarah Doudney
The Snow Witch, by Matt Wingett

Non-Fiction:
Conan Doyle and the Mysterious World of LIght, Matt Wingett
From Prison Dock to Portsmouth Dockyard*, Anon
Portchester Castle, Its Origin, History and Antiquities*, Anon
Recollections of John Pounds, Henry Hawkes
Ten Years In A Portsmouth Slum, Robert Dolling
The Autobiography of Sir Walter Besant*, Sir Walter Besant
The History of Portsmouth, Lake Allen
The Narrative of the Loss of the Royal George at Spithead, 1782, Anon, 1845

Other Books

Ghost and Ragman Roll, Pete Adams, 2017
A Handbook For Travellers In Surrey, Hampshire And The Isle Of Wight, Anon, 1876
Portsmouth and Southsea Official Guide, Anon, circa 1956
Mansfield Park, Jane Austen, 1814
Penelope Goes To Portsmouth, M C Beaton, 1991
The Saucy Jack, A Blue Jacket, 1840
Heads and Tails, (short story in Portsmouth Fairy Tales for Grown-Ups), Diana Bretherick, 2014
The Restless Tide, Julia Bryant, 2002
Glass, Alex Christofi, 2015
On The Loss Of The Royal George, (Poem), William Cowper, 1782
Observations On A Tour Through Almost The Whole Of England, And A Considerable Part Of Scotland, Charles Dibdin, 1801
Nicholas Nickleby, Charles Dickens, 1839
Portsmouth, article from All The Year Round, September 24th, Charles Dickens, 1859
Charles Dickens As I Knew Him, Sir George Dolby, 1885
Sir Arthur Conan Doyle, Memories And Adventures, 1924
Sir Arthur Conan Doyle, The Stark Munro Letters, 1895
Memoirs Of An Unfortunate Son Of Thespis, Edward Cape Everard, 1818
The Ocean At The End Of The Lane, Neil Gaiman, 2013
Neil Gaiman, The Tragical Comedy And Comical Tragedy Of Mr Punch, 1994
Violent Cases, Neil Gaiman, 1987
The Story of My Experiments With Truth, Mahatma Gandhi, 1927
Pompey 'Til I Die (poem), Katie Gill, 2017
Lifestory, Alison Habens, 2003
Fragments of Voyages and Travels, Second Series, Volume 2, Captain Basil Hall, 1832

Fragments of Voyages and Travels, Third Series, Volume 3, Captain Basil Hall, 1833

The Portsmouth Road, Charles G Harper, 1895

A Girl Called Thursday, Lilian Harry, 2002

A Promise To Keep, Lilian Harry, 2003

Cut To Black, Graham Hurley, 2004

Rules of Engagement, Graham Hurley, 1990

Westward Ho!, Charles Kingsley, 1855

Baa Baa Black Sheep (short story), Rudyard Kipling, 1888

Something of Myself, Rudyard Kipling, 1937

The Light That Failed, Rudyard Kipling, 1895

The Dark Beneath, J S Law, 2015

Peter Simple, Captain F Marryat, 1834

Pompey, Jonathan Meades, 1993

Evan Harrington, George Meredith, 1860

The Red Sailor, Patrick O'Hara, 1963

Notes On The West Indies, George Pinckard, 1806

Beatrix Potter's Journal, Beatrix Potter, abridged by Glen Cavaliero, 1986

Voyage In The Dark, Jean Rhys, 1934

Death Lies Beneath, Pauline Rowson, 2012

The Suffocating Sea, Pauline Rowson, 2008

Heartstone, C J Sansom, 2010

Things To Do Around Southsea, Maggie Sawkins, poem from This Island City, 2010

Sisters By The Sea, Clement Scott, 1897

Landfall, Nevil Shute, 1940

Requiem For A Wren, Nevil Shute, 1955

So Disdained, Nevil Shute, 1928

A Study In Southsea, Geoffrey Stavert, 1987

The Secret of the Scarlet Ribbon, Justin Strain, 2017

Lawless and the House of Electricity, William Sutton, 2017

Lawless and the Three Pompey Piglets, William Sutton, (short story in Portsmouth Fairy Tales for Grown-Ups), 2014

Experiments In Autobiography, H G Wells, 1934

The History of Mr Polly, H G Wells, 1910

The Dreadnought Of The Air, Percy F Westerman, 1914

The Young Cavalier, Percy F Westerman, 1911

The Snow Witch, Matt Wingett, 2017

Red on Wight, Diana Winsor, 1972

P G Wodehouse, Uneasy Money, 1916

Portsmouth Papers with literary interest

13 A History of Portsmouth's Theatres, H Sargent, 1971

14 Portsmouth Nineteenth Century Literary Figures, A Temple Patterson, 1972

15 Portsmouth As Others Have Seen It: Part I 1540-1790, Margaret J Hoad, 1972

20 Portsmouth As Others Have Seen It: Part II 1790-1900, Margaret J Hoad, 1973

74 Portsmouth Novelists, David Francis, 2006

Prints from Life Is Amazing

If you would like copies of the art work in this book, please go to the shop at:

www.lifeisamazing.co.uk

A selection of prints in different sizes is available, with many images being available as large prints.

Acknowledgments

Thank you to Dr Alison Habens for your encouragement, ditto to Christine Lawrence, to members of the Memories of Bygone Portsmouth facebook group, including Eileen Kelly for the use of her copy of *The Great Salterns*.

Thanks also to Portsmouth History Centre for your help.

A very big thanks to the many amazing writers in the present day who sent me copies of their books include.

And an apology to any I may have missed.

And thank you, too, to Jackie, who kept coming home to a pile of books on the dining room table that caused us to eat in the garden on more than one occasion.

Maps

Map 1 - The Island and its environs, including the Portsdown Hill,
Landport and Portsea sections of the tour.

Map 2 - Old Portsmouth and the first stop on the Southsea leg
of the tour.

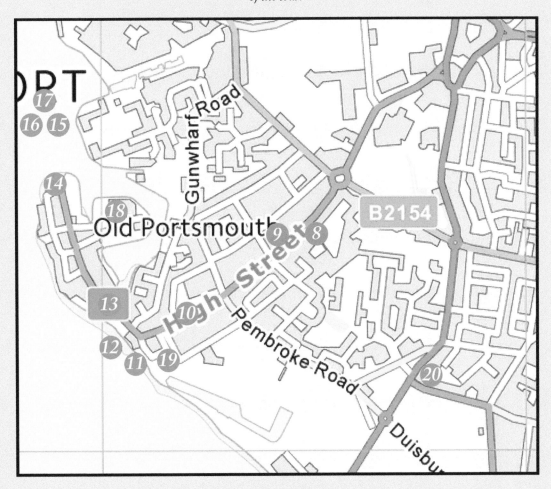

Map 3 - The complete Southsea leg of the tour.

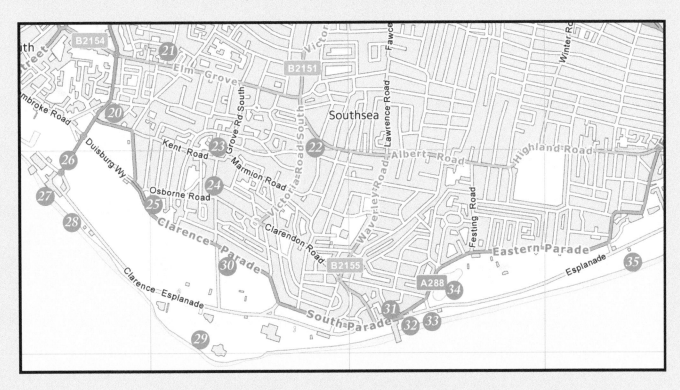

Lightning Source UK Ltd.
Milton Keynes UK
UKHW050744111218
333813UK00003B/23/P

9 780995 639485